TAKEN
AT THE FLOOD

There is a tide in the affairs of men
Which taken at the flood leads on to fortune,
Omitted, all the voyage of their life
Is bound in shallows and in miseries.

JULIUS CAESAR, 4.3.216

by

PATRICK DEVLIN

(edited by Madeleine, Tim & Angela Devlin
with help from other members of the family)

Contributions from
Cardinal Hume
Sir Ludovic Kennedy and Lord Scarman

Copyright Tim Devlin Enterprises (TDE). All rights reserved.
No part of this book may be reproduced,
stored in any retrieval system or transmitted in any form
or by any means without the prior permission of TDE.

Published 1996 by Taverner Publications
Taverner House, East Harling, Norfolk NR16 2QR

Distributed by TDE
Ramsons, Maidstone Road, Staplehurst, Kent TN12 0RD
Tel. 01580 893176

Printed by Postprint
Taverner House, East Harling, Norfolk NR16 2QR

ISBN 1 901470 00 8

APPRECIATION

PATRICK DEVLIN was one of the truly great legal intellects of the 20th century. He excelled in legal practice as a barrister: he excelled as a judge – at all levels: and he was an inspirational jurist.

On 11th August 1992 I wrote a short article for *The Guardian* in which I put the case for Devlin as a champion of justice. In it I said that "his ever-pressing concern was that the law should be just in practice as well as in theory" and that it was his belief "that no law could be just which ignored moral standards."

Whatever he was doing and wherever he found himself – in a court, holding a public inquiry, advising, writing, or in action as a judge or public servant, these were his beliefs. And he fought for them courageously – in public and privately. His courage and his persistence were as remarkable as his intellect.

Taken at the Flood tells the story. It reveals also the hidden strengths of the United Kingdom. Devlin's father was a man of Northern Ireland; his mother was a Scot. He was educated in an English Roman Catholic school of great distinction. He studied at Cambridge University. He became an English barrister, and later an English judge.

Dare I say it? The United Kingdom is a fine nursery for men of the character and talent of Patrick Devlin: and his career shows that Britain gives them the opportunities they need to put their talent to good use in the service of their country.

October 1996   *Lord Scarman*

CONTENTS

INTRODUCTION

"His Majesty's judges", Lord Chief Justice Hewart told a Guildhall banquet before the war, "are well satisfied with the almost universal admiration in which they are held", a view echoed after the war by Lord Chancellor Kilmuir when he said that so long as judges kept silent on non legal matters, "their reputation for wisdom and impartiality will remain unassailable".

Such complacency was anathema to Patrick Devlin and led in the post war years to some judges falling short of the impartiality expected of them, particularly in their reluctance to challenge dubious police evidence, the commonest cause of major miscarriages of justice. Nor when convictions were quashed and appellants freed after years of wrongful imprisonment, did judges show any inclination to express regret for mistakes made and hardship suffered; for, as Patrick says, the simple price of an apology was not one they were willing to pay. No doubt they considered it *infra dig* as well as a further undermining of people's faith in justice. Recently Lord Justice Farquharson did have the grace to apologise to an appellant he had freed and one must hope that others will follow his example.

If I write mainly in the past tense, it is because the old guard of judges have now mostly retired and the new intake seem a different breed. Patrick Devlin never belonged to the old guard, yet always retained their respect. In everything he did or tried to do he was his own man, conformist in the sense that he believed it was not the business of judges to create law but to fashion it, non-conformist in almost everything else: a highly original thinker, many of whose varied interests lay outside the law, a moralist but not an evangelist, a lively conversationalist, a *bon viveur* (it was no accident that on first coming to live in London he chose Mayfair rather than Bloomsbury), an eloquent practitioner of both the written and spoken word, a devoted family man, a latter day farmer; never a seeker of controversy but unafraid of it when it came. His guide for living, he says, was to get the greatest enjoyment out of life and none who knew him would deny that he succeeded.

In this memoir of his early life there is a striking passage in which Patrick says that the motivation of his professional career was the pursuit of virtue:

> The virtue which most like to pursue is charity which can be modernised as social service. The motive which powers it is compassion. For me the virtue is justice which is powered by a colder emotion, the root of which is a love of the order that moves the

5

universe, and which is an aspect of godliness. Compassion and justice are very compatible but, if forced to choose, I would rather be just than compassionate.

Anyone who surveys Patrick's career as a whole must be glad that he never had to choose, that he was always just and compassionate in equal measure; and never more so than in his handling of the trial for murder of Dr John Bodkin Adams, the Eastbourne G.P. who was suspected of bumping off rich, elderly female patients whom he had persuaded to remember him in their wills.

It was on the last day of this trial in 1957 that I saw Patrick in the flesh for the first time. I had gone there on an impulse because although the evidence against the doctor had sounded persuasive at the beginning of the trial, it had become markedly less so as it proceeded; and I wanted to hear how the summing-up would resolve it.

The first thing I noticed was the beauty of Patrick's voice, as modulated and seductive in its own way as that of another great judge, Norman Birkett; and it was sometimes accompanied by the unobtrusive withdrawal of one small, exquisitely formed hand from the voluminous sleeve of his robe to emphasise a point to the jury. The effect was mesmeric, almost like an artistic performance. And then there was the message. A lesser judge, aware that the chief prosecuting counsel was the Attorney-General, Sir Reginald Manningham-Buller (known to the profession as 'Bullying Manner') might have been tempted to give a 'neutral' summing-up. But to Patrick the status of the prosecutor was of no consequence. Unequivocally he told the jury that there was insufficient evidence to convict and they must not construe the doctor's silence as in any way indicative of guilt. That was his alienable right; and accordingly the doctor was acquitted.

Thirty years later Patrick published his book on the case, *Easing the Passing*. It was the first occasion of a former judge making public an account of a trial over which he had presided, and was praised by the critics as an invaluable insight into the workings of a trial judge's mind. Inevitably though his strictures on the competence or rather incompetence, of Manningham-Buller led to mutterings from the old guard of judges. Although Patrick was long retired and Manningham-Buller long dead, they saw the book as a sort of fouling of the judicial nest as well as the betrayal of a professional colleague; to all of which Patrick was quite indifferent.

It was not long after the Bodkin Adams trial that Patrick published his landmark book *The Criminal Prosecution in England*, and thus unwittingly threw me a lifeline. I was then completing my own book on the Christie-Evans murders in which I concluded that Evans would never have been convicted, let alone hanged, if the detectives in charge of the case had not extracted a false 'confession' from him late at night in order to present a cast-iron case. This was an unfashionable, not to say subversive claim, but I knew it to be true, not only in that case but others; and I cannot express the exhilaration I felt on finding confirmation of my beliefs from – of all people – the pen of a High Court Judge:

> When the prosecution seek to put a confession in evidence, the burden is upon them to prove that it was made voluntarily... It is the general habit of the police never to admit to the slightest departure from correctness... Policemen cannot afford to make too many mistakes. They have to be sure of themselves... Often in the past (the jury) must have known that the police account of the way in which the interview was carried out was nonsense... The fault to be looked for today is not the frame-up but the tendency to press interrogation too hard against a man believed to be guilty.

The old guard of judges must have recognised the truth of these observations, so inimical to the pursuit of justice, yet none dared publicly to support them.

In the early 1960s I made two documentary films on the police for the television programme *This Week*, and heartened by Patrick's words and in the light of further miscarriages, I spoke of the police bending the Judges' Rules, especially in relation to 'confessions'. Naturally the old guard were swift to denounce me. "Bending the rules", boomed Manningham-Buller (now elevated to Lord Dilhorne) "seldom occurs" – this from a Lord Chancellor of whom Patrick had written that he had not a grain of judicial sense. Lord Shawcross QC, who had taken part in the programme, thundered, "There is no foundation whatever for such opinions", while Sir Lionel Heald, a former Attorney-General, claimed that the programmes had been faked. All these strictures were of course articles of faith, as not only had none of the old guard studied the matter, but they assumed that nobody else had either.

In the mid 1970s the papers were full of attempts to clear the names of two petty London criminals named McMahon and Cooper who had been sentenced to life imprisonment for the murder of a sub-postmaster in Luton. In fact they were two innocents who had been framed by a senior detective named Commander Kenneth Drury who himself went to prison on corruption charges later. The case was singular in that it had been referred to the Court of Appeal an unprecedented five times. Cooper's M.P., Bryan Magee, had interested Patrick in the case, and he was concerned that justice might have miscarried on a point of law; that while the two men had been convicted by a jury, the judges of the Fourth Court had taken it on themselves to summon the chief prosecution witness, a proven liar and the only one of the gang to have been arrested, to appear before them; and as a result of what he had said, dismissed the appeal. In a forthright lecture given at All Souls College, Oxford, Patrick said that what the Fourth Court should have done was either to have quashed the convictions and ordered a new trial or if that was impractical owing to the lapse of time (the two men had already served seven years) justice demanded that the Court should also have called witnesses for McMahon and Cooper.

I was unaware of Patrick's lecture at the time he delivered it, but coincidentally I was sent manuscripts on the case written in prison by McMahon and Cooper. Together these convinced me that this was one of the worst examples I had yet seen of a deliberate frame-up to pervert the course of justice. While assembling material for a book on the case, I read Patrick's lecture and asked him if he would consider contributing to it.

He suggested a meeting. I suggested lunch which took place at one of Patrick's favourite watering places, the Grillroom of the Connaught Hotel. Looking back, I recall a sense of excitement mingled with slight trepidation at the prospect of sharing meal and a *tête à tête* with a man I had so long admired. However, he (and the vintage claret he recommended) helped to put me at ease, and by the time we parted, he had agreed to contribute two chapters to the book, what he called Foreword and Afterword. Because these are vivid examples of his sense of justice blended with compassion, I give extracts from both:

From the Foreword

> If I thought that due process had been observed in this case, I should not be writing this Foreword and commending this book to the public… Since I have held high judicial office, I have had to consider carefully whether I ought to go any further. There is a sound convention which applies in all walks of life and should apply especially to the judiciary, that the retired should not set up as public fault finders. This has never been taken to ban discussion of trends in the law with those who are professionally and academically interested… But it is quite a different matter to enter into a controversy which is likely to follow an appeal to the public against the decision of the Courts. The temptation to refrain would be irresistible were it not tempered by the conviction that in this case a failure of justice has gone unperceived with catastrophic consequences to two young men. I may wish, as selfishly I do, that I had never taken this particular path or met with this situation; but meeting it, I cannot cross to the other side of the road. If there are any whom I have thereby offended, I express my regret.

And this, from the Afterword, after he had lucidly explained the complex arguments that he led him to say that the judgement of the Fourth Court had been flawed:

> The law is marked out in black and white; men must be guilty or innocent. For the prerogative of mercy which is above the law, there are no such markings. These men have now served more than half of the exemplary sentences passed upon them. It is less than their full desserts if they are guilty, but yet by any standard a drastic punishment. If they are innocent, the thought of another ten years out of their lives is not tolerable. If the Home Secretary now cuts the knot, I do not believe that there is a voice in England that would be raised in protest.

Within three weeks of publication the Home Secretary, Willie Whitelaw, had cut the knot and ordered the men's release, and their ten year ordeal was over. Yet in my view this was not enough and when I met Willie later on holiday I asked why he hadn't recommended a free pardon. "I wanted to", he replied, "but the Lord Chief Justice objected". This ungenerous attitude was typical of the old guard and meant that the two men would never receive compensation for what they had suffered and never be officially cleared.

Eight years later Patrick was faced with the same problem again. In October 1974 the I.R.A. planted bombs in two Guildford public houses which resulted in the deaths of six people and the wounding of fifty others. Public opinion was outraged and there was great pressure on the police to arrest those responsible.

Unfortunately and *pace* Patrick's observations on police malpractice in *The Criminal Prosecution in England*, the pressures proved too much for the police and they arrested the wrong people. The Guildford Four, as they became known were, in Patrick's words 'a pitiable lot', three young Irish drifters and an English girl who had been on drugs since she was eleven. There being no evidence against them worth the name, yet having deluded themselves into believing the Four were guilty, the police resorted to 'strong arm' methods to extract 'confessions'. These the jury accepted and the four were sentenced to life imprisonment.

Between trial and appeal, two of the I.R.A. gang who had planted the Guildford bombs were arrested and tried for planting bombs in Woolwich. Refusing to plead, they complained that they had not also been charged with the Guildford bombings for which four innocent people had been convicted. At the appeal of the Four these two I.R.A. men were called for the appellants, repeated that they and they alone had carried out the Guildford bombings and gave details of how they had done it *which were known only to the police*. Despite this and no doubt reluctant to admit that the law had made another monumental cock-up, the Appeal Court judges ruled that while the I.R.A. men probably had planted the bombs, the convicted four must have been there as well, although 'confessions' apart, there was not a scrap of evidence for it; and their appeals were dismissed.

As in the Luton case what Patrick and others objected to was that once again the Appeal Court had taken on itself the judging of facts, a function that had always been the prerogative of juries. They had been enabled to do this because the House of Lords had decreed that "if the Appeal Court has no reasonable doubt about the verdict, the Court does not think the jury could have one". In a powerful article in *The Times* Patrick and Lord Scarman, the two outstanding judges of their generation, called this 'an astounding proposition'; for had a new jury heard the old 'confession' evidence together with the exculpatory evidence of the I.R.A. men, they must surely have had grave doubts about the safety of the conviction. In his epilogue to this book Cardinal Hume relates how he, Patrick, Leslie Scarman and two former Home Secretaries, Merlyn Rees and Roy Jenkins, were so concerned about the case that they called the Home Secretary of the day to consider it afresh; and so the way was paved for the eventual release of the Four, fifteen years after their wrongful conviction.

If there was any post-war judge whose character, intellect, integrity and natural authority fitted him for the posts of either Lord Chief Justice or Master of the Rolls, it was surely Patrick Devlin. Unfortunately for him the time was out of joint, the then incumbents staying on longer than expected, and after brief spells as a Lord Justice of Appeal and as a Law Lord, whose cases he said, bored him unutterably, he retired at the early age of 58. Yet he had left his mark; as Chairman of a variety of government Commissions and Inquiries, for his handling of the Bodkin Adams case, and also in finding time to write three influential books on the philosophy of the law: *Trial by Jury*, *The Criminal Prosecution in England* and *Samples of Lawmaking*.

With time on his hands after retirement, he took on the chairmanship of other bodies such as the Press Council and the Joint Board for the newspaper industry; became a judge of the Administrative Tribunal of the I.L.O. and as an arbitrator in cases of dispute between multi-national companies which took him, for handsome rewards, to such agreeable foreign parts as Lisbon and Geneva. He chaired a tribunal of assessors in a famous television debate on Ulster, despite the government having asked the BBC to cancel it; he published more books (*Enforcement of Morals*, *The Judge*, *The Jury in two Constitutions*) and until 1961 kept up his long-standing chairmanship of Wiltshire Quarter Sessions at Salisbury and Devizes, both only a short drive from his house at Pewsey. Here, as was the custom, he abandoned wig and robes for country suitings. The proceedings were more informal than those in the High Court, and London barristers felt it a privilege to appear.

Throughout his long life Patrick's anchor was his family – his wife Madeleine, their four sons and twin daughters and the pretty Georgian house at Pewsey he had bought in 1943 and the farm that went with it. For my wife and myself, living nine miles away, it was always a joy to be invited there, to sample Patrick's superb cellar and to enjoy his and Madeleine's company and that of other like-minded guests. It was here at the age of 82 that Patrick began this memoir of his life, and those of his friends who thought they had already read the last of him will be delighted by this account of early days in Aberdeen and at Cambridge University where he was a notable president of the Union, followed by early years at the Bar. Yet I doubt if they will put the final chapter down without a renewed sense of loss, both for the man himself and for further instalments of a remarkable life which, because of his death, have been denied us.

Patrick Devlin enriched my life and that of many others. It was a rare privilege to have known him.

Ludovic Kennedy

Chapter I

DEVLINS AND CROMBIES

DURING the Easter vacation of 1925 my father told me that it was time that I made up my mind about a profession. I was then 19 and in my second year at Cambridge. It was not a subject on which he had spoken to me before but evidently he took it for granted that my future would not be unprofessional. If it was not a subject to which I had given much thought, neither was it one for which I was quite unprepared. The preparation for a discussion of this sort was usually initiated by my mother who would say that my father was beginning to think that it was time etc. This was a signal to linger in the dining room after the meal was over so that the matter might be conveniently broached.

I had no talent which it would be death to hide. I had not at my school, Stonyhurst, excelled at anything. Nevertheless, I fancied myself as a public performer of some sort. The fancy arose out of the admirable practice of the Jesuits at Stonyhurst in my day in requiring one of the boys to read to them at dinner in the refectory. I have often thought since how much pleasanter it would be if conversation at meals was not permitted to distract attention from food and drink. I do not mind people talking. So the object could be achieved by removing the social obligation to pay attention to what they are saying. But the substitution of a reader to whom the consumer may or may not listen is the better device.

I am not suggesting that the Jesuitical objective was the enjoyment of food and drink. Some of the reading was devotional, the rest was from some suitable book, a biography perhaps. The reading had to be clear and distinct; inaudibility and mispronunciations were at once corrected. This was a sound and practical training in the use of the voice.

There was also at school an elocution prize and I entered for it several times. On the last occasion F. X. Sullivan, who regularly took the leading part in the school plays, (in later life he became quite famous as Monsieur Poirot in Agatha Christie plays) wrote in the school magazine: – 'P. Devlin may possibly become a good political speaker, but he will never learn how to elocute,' or words to that effect.

Then there was a debating society, flourishing and fashionable. A speech was supposed to last from three to five minutes and no notes might be used. The candidate for membership had to make a qualifying speech which satisfied the committee. For one practised only in reading aloud the composition of a speech which had to go on for three minutes was a daunting task. Moreover to remain a member it was necessary to speak every other week.

A friend of mine, Charles Curran, a quiet and ugly boy, was an active member of the debating society. He held advanced views which he was ready to propagate freely in and out of debates. He as good as advocated the nationalisation of the railways; this was in or about 1920, nearly a quarter of a century before the dreaded event occurred. His earnestness in this matter earned him the sobriquet of Bolshie Curran.

Nevertheless, he had gained the respect of all by an incident in which he displayed remarkable sang-froid. At breakfast, when Bolshie was in full flow to the left of some political topic, the boy who was sitting next to him, a stout Belgian called T'Serclaes, told him to shut up. Bolshie ignored this unseemly interruption. T'Serclaes had a plate full of porridge in front of him: he told Curran that, if he did not shut up, he would empty it over his head. Bolshie had faced threats of this sort before and thought he knew when it was safe to call the bluff. He said: – 'Bet you a shilling you don't'. T'Serclaes immediately did.

This was in the refectory, a large hall accommodating almost the whole school. We gazed in horror. The master was at the other end and our table next to the door. Bolshie rose, dripping porridge, and went out. In a miraculously short time he returned looking more or less respectable and with a shilling in his hand which, with a smile, he tendered to T'Serclaes. Then he resumed his flow.

The incident displayed Bolshie not only as stalwart in a crisis but also before and after the crisis as a man of many words. Many words were just what I needed and I applied to him for them. He explained that he was in the trade of writing speeches for neophytes and that his fee was a penny a minute. I thought this reasonable and contracted to have three minutes' worth. He said that the outlawry of notes was easily got over. I was to study carefully his written text and memorise the opening sentence of each paragraph: from this the rest of the text would swiftly flow. I do not remember the subject of the debate, but the first sentence of the opening paragraph I remember to this day: it was, 'Man is a social animal'.

I followed his instructions. But since I only half-believed in the swiftness of the flow, I memorised a good deal of that also. I was admitted to the society, but only, so I was told privately, after a good deal of discussion. Some members of the committee argued that the whole speech had been learnt by heart, which they said was an evasion of the rule against notes.

When after the fortnight had elapsed I was required to speak again, I went again to Bolshie Curran. He explained that his services were now more eagerly sought and that in accordance with the law of supply and demand he must raise his fee to sixpence minimum. The prospect of a sixpenny levy every fortnight drove me to D.I.Y.. There, I found a broader line which went down more easily than Bolshie's elegant and instructive prose and I concluded my school career with a half of the first prize for debating.

By that time Bolshie Curran had left school. More than forty years passed before I met him again. My wife and I were invited to dinner by Jack and Margaret Huntingdon[1], two good friends, to meet an interesting journalist who was also an M.P..

Jack was an artist who wandered into politics far enough to hold junior office in the Attlee government. Both he and Margaret had catholic tastes, so I was only mildly surprised to find that his guest was the Tory member for Uxbridge who talked quietly and effectively about the issues of the day. Rebecca West, who met him about this time, described him as 'a gentle and kindly creature in spite of a ferocious type of ugliness, who was perhaps the best read man in the field of political science in the Fleet Street and House of Commons of his day'.[2]

Eventually something he said struck a spark of memory and I only just stopped myself from saying: – 'Good heavens, you must be Bolshie Curran'. We renewed our acquaintance without going into nomenclature or detail.

By Easter 1925 I had made some headway at the Cambridge Union and had come to think that a political life would be well worth living. I had learnt also that politics was a life for a man who either had what was called 'private means' or who had already made his way. The most approved method of making a way into politics was to take the way of the Bar. This had its own attractions. In the long vacation of 1924 I had studied the lengthy reports in *The Times* of the case of Vacquier who poisoned the husband of the woman who was his mistress and whom he proposed to marry. Mr Justice Avory, a 'hanging judge', presided at the Surrey Assizes. He was a laconic man: the legend was that once when he returned to London from the Western Circuit, he was asked whether he had had a pleasant circuit and replied only: 'I missed a man at Bodmin'. The Attorney-General, Sir Patrick Hastings, and Sir Edward Marshall Hall were for the prosecution and Sir Henry Curtis-Bennett for the defence. These were great names.

So I said to my father, who was an architect, that I would like to go to the Bar. He said that it was a very fine profession and there the matter ended. I do not suppose that he had any idea of what was involved in getting to the Bar or in making a living when one got there; certainly my own notion was sparse.

But I suppose that we both knew that it depended entirely on Uncle George.

My father, William John Devlin, was pure Irish. The Devlins (to use the modern spelling of a name which, like most names that go back into the centuries, has taken different forms) were one of the septs or clans who from time immemorial had lived in Tyrone in Ulster. The Reformation came; England, save for some remote parts in the North, and Scotland, except for the Highlands, embraced

---

[1] The Countess of Huntingdon who wrote under the name of Margaret Lane.

[2] *Sunday Telegraph*, 19 December 1982. In Robert Rhodes James, *Anthony Eden*, George Weidenfeld & Nicolson, 1986, there is between pp. 426 & 427 a picture of Curran the candidate standing on the hustings beside the Prime Minister. He is not as handsome as Sir Anthony, but he looks very pleasant.

Protestantism. Ireland remained universally Catholic. For the first part of the 16th century the clans fought England and Scotland for their independence and their faith. When the Earl of Tyrone, head of the great clan O'Neill, was humbled, the Donnelys, the Hagans, the Quinns, the Devlins and the other septs had likewise to make their peace. The peace resulted in the Plantations whereby the Catholic proprietors were dispossessed and unrebellious Protestants 'planted' on their lands.

Tyrone was divided into five 'precincts'. The most westerly of them was the precinct of Dungannon, the chief town in that part. The lands around it, including the habitations of Stewartstown, Coalisland and Donaghmore ran to the shores of Lough Neagh. This was the territory known as Mounterevlin, which the Devlins had owned and on which thereafter they subsisted. Until the emigrations that followed the Great Famine they were hardly to be found anywhere else. After that, like the Irish generally, they went to wherever they could find a living, to the new countries overseas, America and Australia, or to the growing cities of Britain, Liverpool and Glasgow. My great-grandfather, Matthew, took himself and his family, which then or later consisted of a wife and six children, from Donagmore, first to Roseneath on the Gare Loch off the Firth of Clyde; and then to Glasgow.

There he founded with his sons a firm of builders in Maclean Street off Paisley Road. The elder son, John, born in 1832, settled down with a wife happily in Glasgow. He bought a house, 37 St Andrew's Drive in Pollokshields. They had three sons and four daughters. One son was killed in the First War and one daughter took the veil. The other children never married. They lived on at No. 37, inseparable in family life, each earning his or her own living save for the daughter who kept house, until the last of them died in the '50s. I used sometimes to break my journey there on the way to school and back.

Daniel, Matthew's youngest child born in 1838, was my grandfather. He was the only one of the children to return to his native land. One sister married a Quinn and went to Chicago; another a MacBride and went to Australia; the others remained in Glasgow. I do not know what took Daniel back to Ireland or when. He bought a house two miles from Coalisland called Rowan Lodge; his children had pleasant memories of it. He owned a business, variously described as a fireclay or cement works, but it was not a great success. The family were remembered in Coalisland for their looks. Daniel and his four children of whom my father, William, was the eldest, were tall and handsome. Unfortunately the genes which controlled the appearance of the males were recessive.

My grandmother died at the age of 39 in 1884 when my father was 14. This event, or perhaps the lack of prosperity, disintegrated the family. The younger children were sent to live with relatives. My father left school at the age of 16. He went to London where he began to qualify as an architect. He did not return to Ireland.

My father was an uncommunicative man. He never talked to us children of his family, of Ireland and his early days, or his work. There was never any question of any of us following in his footsteps.

In my limited experience of Irishmen I have found them to be of two contrasting kinds. The kind which sustains the popular image is extrovert, gregarious, talkative, quick-witted and with a touch of blarney. I have never heard any I have met say *bedad* or *begorrah*, but perhaps there are some who do. The other kind, no less distinctive, is thin, with a long face and keen features, quiet and courteous sometimes in an old-fashioned way and very, very reserved. My father was one of these.

I know little or nothing about him in the period from 1886 to 1900. Since he was diligent and competent, I suppose that, after he qualified, he earned a decent salary in the offices in London in which he worked. I do not suppose that he ever had much to spare, when I knew him, he had that carefulness with money that is bred in those who have had to count their pennies. I know of only one place where he lived; the address on his marriage certificate in 1900 is 12 Gray's Inn Square. Living there, he would have been beside the gate into Gray's Inn Road. In those days the 'pairs', as they were called, consisted, as in Oxford and Cambridge colleges, of a pair of rooms on either side of a staircase. When modern requirements had to be met, conveniences were set up in spaces extracted from one of the rooms. The pairs were leased or allotted to a Bencher who would often sublet. The rent was small. I do not know whether my father lived at No. 12 for a long or a short time. When I was admitted to the Inn as a student in 1925 he made no comment.

In 1897 some work took him to South Africa. On the voyage home in the spring of 1898 there were on board two Miss Crombies, daughters of a wealthy cloth manufacturer. They were in their middle or late twenties and on the second part of a winter voyage to South Africa and back; such voyages were the precursors of the modern cruises. There was a shipboard romance. My father proposed to the younger Miss Crombie (Frances) and was refused, but not in no uncertain terms. She was attracted, but she had doubts about marriage. She gave him a book inscribed: – 'To Will from Fanny. RMS Dunvegan Castle. April 1898'. The book was *Virginibus Puerisque*, a collection of essays by Robert Louis Stevenson, first published in 1881. The copy she gave was the 18th edition printed in 1897. Probably she bought it as soon as she got home. The first four essays are all about marriage.

The Crombies from whom Fanny, my mother, came were lowland Scots with an ancestry as untainted as the Irishry of my father. John Crombie was born at Chapel of Garioch in Aberdeenshire in 1778[1]. It would be speculative to go back further except to say that John's father was called James; John's christening either

---

[1] *"Crombies of Grandholm & Cothal"*, Ed. John R. Allen, Central Press, Aberdeen, p. 22."

inaugurated or continued a practice whereunder the first name of the eldest son in each generation alternated between James and John, the second son being given the name that the elder had not appropriated.

The John born in 1778 worked at Cothal where he had a textile mill, a product of the Industrial Revolution. In 1809 he wedded Catherine Harvey of Monykeppoch. Their elder son, James, came promptly in 1810, but they had to wait another nine years for John. Miss Harvey had been perhaps in a higher walk of life and maybe brought with her a bit of money. Her mother was a Lumsden of Belhelvie and her great niece, Catherine Lumsden, was to marry a Paton of Grandholm. They lived at the Old Manse at Fintray. All these places are in a small stretch of country ten to fifteen miles north of Aberdeen.

The mill specialized in fine quality tweeds. A Crombie overcoat is still something that is talked of. There were bad times in the 1820s. John Crombie was in partnership which in 1828 was dissolved. James, his elder son, was then eighteen and he seems to have come to the fore. The name J. and J. Crombie, now quite a famous trademark, – you can see it advertised in the glossy magazines – may date from then.

Times were still bad in 1837 when James, by now twenty-seven years old, found a suitable bride in Katherine Scott Forbes who brought to the altar about £10,000. The money came from 50,000 Bombay rupees bequeathed to her as a child by her father, Theodore Forbes.

This connection of the Crombies with the great family of Forbes was irregular. Certainly Theodore himself belonged to the branch of the family settled at Boyndlie in Aberdeenshire. In 1808 he obtained a position as a writer in the East India Company. In such a position there was money to be made. In the 1830s Macaulay, the great historian, went to India as legal adviser to the Supreme Council at a salary of £10,000 a year. He held the post for four years and saved enough to make him independent for life. Theodore was not in the same class, but when he died, at the early age of 32 in 1820, he left more than a lakh of rupees (a guess would make it between £10,000 and £15,000) for his dependants. Though he was not a marrying man, he did not shirk his natural obligations. He made provision for a baby he had left behind in Aberdeenshire as well as an annuity for life for his Bombay mistress, and substantial sums for the two children he had by her.

The business at Cothal continued to grow. James, the elder brother, stayed near the mill and bought or built a house at Goval Bank which slopes down steeply to the river Don. John moved nearer to Aberdeen at Balgownie Lodge by the old bridge of Don. James and Katherine had two sons and several daughters. In accordance with the laws discovered by the Abbé Mendel some showed more than others the Indian strain. Their eldest son John, born the year after their marriage, was very swarthy. I was familiar with a portrait of him by Brough[1] that hung at Goval. With his bushy black eyebrows and whiskers he looked like one of the more disreputable characters in the Old Testament. As a young man he was, until his forties, a forceful character in the business. He moved it nearer to Aberdeen, building a larger factory at Grandholm and nearby a house for himself and his family at Woodside, which had become even in my time a suburb of Aberdeen.

John was my mother's father, known to the family as Papa and to the mill as Black Jock. He retired from the business in 1880 with some trouble in the lungs which sent him from time to time to warmer climates. The winter after he retired he took a house in San Remo and then for a while a house at Cheltenham, where my mother was sent to school. When at Danestone (home of Black Jock and family near Aberdeen) he entertained a lot but only relatives and business friends. An indication of the scale of his hospitality is that he laid down a pipe (about 56 dozen bottles), of port wine, Sandeman 1890. Among the business friends was a Mr McQueen, a director of the local railway whose four initials were once stamped on my mind but are now forgotten.

Papa was not by all accounts a very nice man. He was excessively selfish, he treated his wife and children, four sons and four daughters, in the high Victorian fashion. His wife's death in 1893 at the age of 54 left him free for regular as well as irregular pursuits. Within the regular classification the particular quarry was Mr McQueen's daughter Alice. She was the same age as Papa's elder daughters and not much favoured by them, while Uncle George, Papa's third son, then in his early twenties, described her as buxom and goodlooking. The courtship began in 1897, and it may have been to get them out of the way that Papa sent two of his daughters on the cruise to South Africa which ended in Fanny's doubts about matrimony. It was Papa's treatment of his wife and his behaviour generally that was one cause of the doubts. The other cause had been created the year before. Neither cause has anything to do with the theme of this book, but taken together they compose a period piece if such fascination that it would be pedantic to exclude them as irrelevant.

There was in Aberdeen a young man, Duncan Abel, starting in practice at the Scottish Bar. Through some connection he was received at Danestone. In that house, and doubtless in the drawing room when young men called, there were four daughters all of marriageable age. The family was spaced so that the block of daughters, separated in age only by the customary Victorian intervals between births, intervened *en masse* between the eldest son, Jim, and his three brothers, John, George and Theodore. Grace, the eldest daughter, was kind and plain and

[1] *Robert Brough A.R.S.A. (1872-1905)*

out of the running; Connie, who came next was the acknowledged beauty; Fanny, forthcoming and easy on the eye; and Joan, or Janny as she was called, pretty but gauche. How under the conventions of the time was Duncan to disclose his preference for Connie in a way that would best promote its return? There was no mother to guide and contrive; Papa, I am sure, was worse than useless.

It was a situation which seems laughable today but which Jane Austen would have plotted convincingly. Indeed, the social mores in Britain *circa* 1900 resembled far more closely the mores *circa* 1800 than they are likely to resemble those that are to come *circa* 2000. Duncan may have hesitated before he fixed on Connie, thus arousing emotion in other breasts. It is, I suppose, conceivable that, like Frank Churchill in Emma, he dissembled so as to conceal his aims. Or perhaps Fanny was too hopeful or Duncan too clumsy. However it was, when Duncan and Connie were married towards the end of 1896, Fanny temporarily, and Janny permanently, were left with the feeling that men were deceivers ever. Perhaps Fanny's disappointment was another reason for the cruise.

By the summer of 1898 the climax of Papa's courtship was drawing near. The railway company had built a hotel at Cruden Bay up the coast towards Peterhead. There was a luncheon party to celebrate the opening with a special train to take the guests. They included Papa and Alice McQueen. Mr McQueen, evidently playing a large part in the wooing, made a speech in which he referred to the links between the McQueens and the Crombies and to his hope that they would become closer. Papa had in fact proposed several times and Alice was thought to have given an evasive answer. Among Papa's papers after his death there was found a letter refusing him. But perhaps Papa, like Mr Collins in *Pride and Prejudice*, 'was not now to learn that it is usual with young ladies to reject the addresses of the man whom they secretly mean to accept when he first applies for their favour.' Moreover there were other McQueen daughters on the market and Alice was 29; what further opportunities would she get of avoiding spinsterhood and genteel poverty. Mr McQueen was anxious.

The last act was dramatic. Papa prepared for it by ordering diamonds from a London jeweller which he intended to lay before her. (The aria in the jewel scene from Gounod's *Faust* suggests itself here). It was now September and the meeting for the great temptation was fixed for a Monday at the McQueen home. At dinner on the Saturday evening Papa was exceptionally genial. He rose early and went to his desk where he prepared a codicil to his will leaving Alice £10,000. Such an addition to the jewels would be an earnest of the handsome settlement that the bride's father would be poised to negotiate.

On the Sunday morning the children presented themselves in accordance with routine. Papa did not himself go to church on account, he said, of his deafness, but the children had to go, though what church they went to did not matter . So my Uncle George was astonished when Papa said. 'I suppose you're not going to church this morning'.

In the evening Papa felt not very well, perhaps because of the excitement, and went to bed early. But on Monday morning he was no better and sent messages of postponement to Alice. On the Wednesday he became unconscious. The doctor came and said that there was nothing to be done. Papa's younger brother, my great-uncle Teddy, came and said that the Mr (later Sir David) Ferrier, a distinguished neuropathologist, should be sent for from Edinburgh. He came and went, leaving a bill for 300 guineas. For six weeks Papa lay inert, the heavy breathing associated with his condition audible to all who passed the door. On 2 November he died.

I doubt if anyone deeply regretted his death. Uncle Theodore, the youngest of my four Crombie uncles, (perhaps to symbolize the Forbes connection Theodore was now rivalling John and James as a name in the family christenings) told me that his sole concern was that Papa should linger until the first day of the month; his death before then would automatically cancel the next instalment of Theodore's small allowance.

As for Alice, her prudent conduct had produced for her a competence to sustain her spinsterhood. She never married.

Even after the subtraction of the £10,000 and the 300 guineas, Papa's estate was substantial. His 'testamentary dispositions'. (i.e. his will, but it was the feeling of the age that subjects touching on death were better described in polysyllabics) were set out with verbosity and without punctuation in a huge document which I once perused. In the *Twelfthly* paragraph Papa divided the residue among his children. The upper and middle classes did not practise primogeniture but neither were they altogether indiscriminating. In principle girls should get less than boys; they would either get husbands to maintain them or would lead as unmarried women in-expensive lives. So far this was in accordance with principle. But also Papa was angry with the girls, (except Connie, his favourite, who had already been provided for on her marriage) because, he said, they left him in his widowerhood 'like a rat in a hole'.

I dare say that they did not do much to comfort him. My mother had an album of sentimental songs, one of which was called *Alice, Where Art Thou?*[1] which they sang more frequently than was appropriate. Of course, if Papa was too deaf to go to church, he might also have been too deaf to identify the song. Nevertheless, it was provocative. Fortunately for the girls the Scots law of *legitim*, or 'bairns' part' as it is colloquially known, puts a curb on posthumous parental resentment. Under it the children can claim that a minimum of one third of the testator's personal property is apportioned among them equally.

[1] A song composed by one Alfred Bunn who died in 1860; who also composed 'I dreamt that I dwelt in marble halls'.

A difficulty arose over whether or not the pipe of port was an 'appurtenance' of the house and so not personal; George was the only one interested, so it went to the establishment which John and he were setting up together. The girls had legacies from their mother. When eventually everything was settled up, my mother had an income of about £600 or £700 a year. Most of her capital was invested in railway shares and tied up in a trust. It was a very good income for a single person and not bad for a couple. Income tax was 8d in the pound and the pound then was worth forty times what it is today. It was an excellent arrangement provided only that the pound retained its purchasing power and no Victorian could imagine that it might not.

Chapter II

CHISLEHURST

CHISLEHURST is now a shapeless district in outer London. At the beginning of the century it was, if we are to believe Dr Watson, a village surrounded by the 'narrow country lanes' of Kent.

> *"It was on a bitterly cold and frosty morning during the winter of '97 that I was wakened by a tugging at my shoulder. It was Holmes."*
>
> *Ten minutes later they were both in a cab on their way to Charing Cross Station. When they had taken their places in the Kentish train Holmes drew from his pocket a note from Inspector Hopkins dispatched at 3.30 that morning from the Abbey Grange. The writing showed considerable agitation from which Holmes inferred that Sir Eustace was dead. They arrived at Chislehurst Station whence a drive of a couple of miles through narrow country lanes brought them to the park gate.*[1]

It was on 20 September 1900 that my parents were married and Chislehurst was where they went to live. I do not know when my mother wrote the deciding letter but I suspect that it was not very long before; after the decision that brought them together again had been taken there could be no reason for delay. My mother could now bring to the marriage an income which transformed it financially. I am sure that my father would never have proposed if he was not earning enough to make marriage possible, but between possibility and plenty there is a great gap. The consciousness that there would now be plenty must have contributed to my mother's decision to marry. She was never a spendthrift, but she liked spending and indulging in small extravagances. With my father, she began with a big one.

My father was past thirty and had not, I think, made even a small impact in his profession. In an office he probably worked as one of a team in which I do not think he would have shone. He liked working individually and at his own pace, very thoroughly but very slowly. His wife could now give him the facility to work on his own. So they began what they doubtless thought would be a voyage to success by jettisoning his salaried position. Architecture is a profession with opportunities for the gifted individual since the great prizes are often thrown open to competition. So he took an office in London and set to work. My mother did not do this for him by providing him with money for his office expenses. She simply put the whole of her income into a joint account. It was a trust which he never abused.

[1] The Complete Sherlock Holmes Short Stories. London, John Murray (1928) p. 833.

In Chislehurst they led a surburban life in a small house with a garden looked after by a jobbing gardener who came once or twice a week. They had a bathroom and a W.C., but otherwise their lack of modern conveniences might today have put them below the poverty line. No car of course in 1900 and they were not 'carriage folk', as Fanny had been at Danestone. No telephone, radio nor television. But in relation to the things that the elderly and old fashioned still think to be the things that matter most, they were rich indeed. A cook and a housemaid, costing together about £50 a year and their keep, in a shared room at the top of the house. Elegant furniture which my father knew how to choose and which would fetch a high price today. As many books as they wanted and plenty of room for bookshelves; a circulating library. A piano which all young ladies like my mother had been taught to play. Tradesmen who called for orders and delivered at the back door. A good train service to London for a shopping day or on a Saturday afternoon for a matinée at the theatre. What my parents most liked were the promenade concerts at the Queen's Hall started by Henry Wood in 1895: admission to standing room cost a shilling.

My mother made friends quite easily among the ladies with comparable leisure. They went to tea parties at each others' houses, followed perhaps by card games. Since the guests could not unhatted leave their own houses, the hostess would match them by coming down from upstairs wearing a hat too, even, my mother said, fixing it securely with hat pins. I suppose that there were dinner parties. My father was not fond of social life, but he did not evade it.

In January 1904 the first child was born, a girl; in November 1905 a boy, me; in May 1907 another boy and in April 1909 another girl. Four children; and in eight years not, so far as I know, a single substantial client, nor any success in the numerous competitions at which my father worked hard.[1]

Financially the children hardly mattered. Nurses and nursemaids were easy to get. Beattie came when I was born. I do not remember her at all then, but she was a delightful woman when I met her again forty years later. My mother was very fond of her and once told me the following story. Beattie had taken me out in a perambulator for the customary airing. She stopped outside a shop to make a purchase. The shop was on the edge of a paved area which sloped down to an ornamental pool. When she came out of the shop, Beattie was horrified to see the perambulator, which she could not have securely parked, gliding downwards, while some boys on a seat by the pool were loudly laughing at the prospect of what they took to be an empty perambulator ending its journey in the water. Beattie shouted

---

[1] William and Frances did in fact have five living children (see page 35). The eldest Joan Mary and the second youngest Frances became nuns. Christopher, the second son, became a Jesuit scholar and missionary who wrote a number of books including a life of Robert Southwell SJ and edited The Sermons and Devotional writings of Gerard Manley Hopkins. William, the youngest, born in 1911, became well-known as a Shakespearean actor.

and ran; one of the boys jumped up and pulled the perambulator into safety. Shaken, Beattie went straight back home and at once confessed to my mother the deplorable story. 'Beatrice', my mother said, 'if I had heard about this from any lips except yours, I should have dismissed you at once; but since you have owned up, I shall forgive you'.

Four children in the nursery was one thing and four children with school bills to be paid another. My father regretted all his life that he had not had a thorough education. Master O'Rafferty's school at Coalisland does not seem to have been up to much and anyway he finished schooling at sixteen. He regretted his ignorance of the classics and in his fifties he was taking lessons in French. I think that it was Mr Pott, the editor of *The Eatanswill Gazette* who wrote a leading article on Chinese metaphysics which Mr Pickwick much admired; and who, when asked how he had come by such a store of knowledge, replied that he first looked up China in the British Encyclopedia and then Metaphysics and combined the information. My father seems to have favoured a similar operation. Among his books, I found three leather-bound volumes of the works of Tacite, Cicero and Lucrece, the texts in Latin and the translations in French.

The art of making money is part of the art of enterprise. The man of talent, who is deficient in enterprise, may still do very well in institutional life – the civil service or the great commercial organizations where salaries are paid according to a scale. Or he can join a partnership in which one partner at least knows how to turn talent, his own or another's, into money. My father disliked institutions and was lukewarm about partners. An idea that he might join forces with his cousin John, who practised as an architect in Glasgow and had some of the business sense my father lacked, came to nothing. I do not mean that he could not run an office efficiently, but that he had no sense of how to get business and keep it. An author can get himself a literary agent and an actress an impresario. In the law solicitors have partnerships and barristers have clerks. There will be more to be said in this book about barristers' clerks: I for one, not being an entrepreneur, should have been lost without one.

Until quite recently it was generally thought that success in life for all but the most talented and forceful characters depended greatly upon the influence of family or friends. It may have been this idea that turned my parents' thoughts towards Aberdeen. They heard, moreover, that there were prospects there as well as influence. It was probably on a visit to Aberdeen (for the Crombies had certainly not disintegrated and my mother kept up all her family contacts) that they met Father Meany, the Administrator of the Roman Catholic Cathedral at Aberdeen and a power in the diocese: he was soon to become a Monsignor and the Vicar-General.

There were of course architects in Aberdeen but none of them was a Catholic. There is, or was, a feeling that it was slightly impious for the churches, chapels, convents and even the houses of the clergy to be constructed or altered according to the designs of a heretic. There was also the practical feeling that, since Catholics were still aliens in Presbyterian Scotland and so at a disadvantage in the competition for work and trade, work generated within the congregation should be reserved for its members. At any rate Father Meany was definitely of the opinion that a Catholic architect was needed in Aberdeen.

So in 1909 after the birth of the fourth child the move to Aberdeen was decided upon. The long railway journey was made by night when the children could be put to sleep. The recollection marks for me the dawn of memory. Beattie stayed with us until the resettlement was completed. Then she left to fulfil her engagement to her 'follower', Albert Bevington, a footman in the establishment at Badminton[1] of the Duke of Beaufort. She came to tea with us half a century later when Albert was the Duke's steward, and I was the judge on circuit at Bristol, in the judge's lodgings.

[1] He served Queen Mary when she stayed there during World War II.

Chapter III

ABERDEEN

ABERDEEN is a city built of granite between the mouths of two rivers, the Dee and the Don, flowing into the North Sea. Both rivers rise in the Cairngorms, which are the Highlands west of the city and flow from west to east, the Don north of the Dee; in their approach to the city the Don turns south and the Dee north so that their mouths are separated by only a couple of miles of coast. Both rivers are very beautiful. I have since as a visitor been to country perhaps more beautiful in Ireland, but the Dee and the Don are part of my youth. The Dee is the better known because there is a railway running alongside it to Ballater and thence a road that goes to Balmoral Castle and then to Braemar. Before the days of the motor coach the railway was suburban as far as Culter, passing Milltimber on the way and then taking what seemed to be great strides to Banchory, Aboyne, Dinnet and then Ballater forty miles away.

The city of Aberdeen began by the bridge of Don, where it is still called Old Aberdeen, and spread southwards to the Dee and westwards to the hills. J. & J. Crombie belonged to Donside. James had his home at Goval on the Don and John at Balgownie near its mouth. The Scots seem tender to unmarried daughters; Papa left Danestone to his elder son Jim or, if he did not want it, to his unmarried daughters. Jim did not want it, neither did the daughters, so it was sold. Papa left Goval, where two of his sisters, Maggie and Kate, were living, to his second son John.

John the elder, that is, James's younger brother, had two sons at least; I heard of a third, but he was said to be a black sheep who had disappeared. The older son, John William, inherited Balgownie Lodge and the younger, James Edward, acquired a large mansion at Parkhill which lies between Dyce and Goval.

John William, if he had lived longer, might have been the most distinguished of the Crombies. He became the Liberal member of Parliament for Kincardine and private secretary to the great Lord Bryce who shone in both the political and the academic firmaments. He married the daughter of a Liberal Privy Councillor and had a house in South Kensington as well as Balgownie Lodge. Although Papa's first cousin, he was, because the first John was ten years younger than the first James, almost as near in age to Papa's children. My mother had happy recollections of him taking her, to the disapproval of some Crombies, to see Mrs Patrick Campbell in *The Second Mrs Tanqueray*. That must have been in 1893. John William died in 1908

26

at the age of 51, but his wife, Cousin Minna, lived on for many years in both houses where she liked to entertain.

These were all from John's side of the J. & J. From James' side there was another son, my great-uncle Teddy, who lived with his family at Culter House. James had also various daughters, my great-aunts; I remember only one of them, Aunt Maggie, who was one of the two living at Goval. There was at least one more sister who had a daughter called Ruth, who though she was nearly a decade younger than my mother was her favourite cousin. Ruth married in 1898 Cousin Willie Gill, an army officer; he retired as a colonel in 1910 but remained active in the Territorials. They had a family of two sons and three most attractive daughters and lived at Dalhebity, a house with a lovely garden at Bieldside just out of Aberdeen.

All these Crombies and their friends moved in the 'first circles' of Aberdeen society on the fringe of the County Families. So for us children as we grew up there was no lack of parties. We were of course the poor relations, entertained and not expected to ask back, but were never made to feel embarrassed by this. These were all families in the outer ring of our lives. The inner ring, the uncles and aunts, Papa's children, played a more intimate part. Only two uncles and one aunt lived in Aberdeen but the others kept in close touch by correspondence and visits. Aberdeen remained the meeting place and for most of them the centre of their webs.

Uncle Jim, the eldest, married a girl with an ambition to enter London Society. So he took over the London office of J. & J. Crombie in Golden Square. He made business visits to Aberdeen and retained his membership of the Royal Northern, the club in Union Street, to which the elite of town and county belonged. The Crombies thought membership essential. Jim insisted on Theodore, the youngest brother, who had no intention of residing in Aberdeen, joining the club; he even made a special visit from London to make sure of his election. Theodore said it was the only occasion on which he entered the club. It was in Aberdeen that Jim died in 1921.

The excursion into Society was not unsuccessful, though it was slow going before 1914 and after 1914 disappointing when Society began to lose its capital S and infiltration changed into flood. The children married well. The oldest daughter, Jean, always called in on us when, with her first husband, she visited their friends in the country, such as the Barclay-Harveys of Dinnet. When through no fault on either side that marriage broke down, she married a French baron[1] and herself became a Frenchwoman in thought and deed as well as in nationality.

Jim's only son, Harvey, entered the Navy and retired as a Rear-Admiral. Their younger daughter, christened Helen but by what I have always thought of as a

[1] Baron de Boulemont (see page 86).

misfortune, called Kitten, married a naval friend of her brother's and he retired as a Vice-Admiral[1] and a Knight. All this was very satisfactory. Uncle Jim served rather than shared his wife's social ambitions and remained a delightful man.

Not long after the First War was over Jim and Letty, (she had changed her name from Charlotte which was going out of fashion[2]), came with Kitten to spend a holiday at the Fife Arms in Braemar. We too were there, spending a summer holiday in rooms over the grocer's shop by the Cluanie Bridge. Uncle Jim was an energetic walker and I went out with him a lot and sometimes lunched with him at the Fife Arms.

In later life I saw more of Uncle Jim's house in London than I did of him or his family. In the 1920s he lived at 30 Hans Place. A decade or so later I visited it often, for the girl I was to marry lived there. Several decades after that a colleague in the House of Lords invited my wife and myself to dine with him at his *pied-a-terre* in London. The *pied-a-terre*, sitting-room, bedroom, bathroom and kitchen spread itself over most, if not all, of the drawing-room of 30 Hans Place.

After Jim there came the four sisters. The first and fourth never married; each had an income sufficient to support a less pecunious friend and so they did. Grace's friend, ten years older than she, was a lively little woman called May Robinson. She had several sisters and a brother called Beasley Robinson who, I believe, was a housemaster at Eton. Someone had left Beasley £50,000; it was thought that he ought to 'do something' for his sisters, but he never did. There were many conversations beginning:– 'Beasley is the sort of man who…'. Grace was a melancholy and kindly woman but her kindnesses were of an improving sort not very attractive to children, such as a visit to an art gallery or the offer of a present conditional upon 'being good'.

Janny was an active and intelligent woman. She thought that she ought to do something in life and became a nurse. But she too set up with a woman older than herself, the matron of the nursing home where she worked, called first Maud and then Lucy. (I suppose that Tennyson's poem, *Come into the garden*, led to a surplus of Mauds; Lady Cunard, a celebrated hostess of the thirties, changed her name from Maud to Emerald). Lucy shared Janny's distrust of men but with more justification for she had been jilted by a doctor who decided to marry for money.

So Grace and Janny never lived in Aberdeen though they were assiduous correspondents and came often on visits when they stayed with Connie. She was the lynchpin of the family structure while George became the finial. Uncle Duncan died early in the century, it was said from an illness caused by damp sheets in the

[1] Vice Admiral Peveril William-Powlett, KCB, KIMG, CBE, DSO and Governor of Southern Rhodesia November 1954-December 1959.

[2] But by 1986 it was back in fashion, heading *The Times* popularity poll for newly born females.

hotels where he stayed in pursuit of his practice as a young barrister. So early in life Connie became a widow with a small son, christened John Duncan and called Dick.

When my father moved to Aberdeen in 1909 he rented a house in the Rubislaw district and later bought a house at 60 Rubislaw Den North. The Den was an area of 10 or 20 acres of wooded country through which there ran a fast moving burn. When the area was developed, the Den was left in the middle with houses on the north and south sides which had garden gates leading into it. Aunt Connie had a house at 43 Rubislaw Den South while John and George led together a bachelor existence higher up at number 64. John was the more avuncular of the two. He gave us all half a sovereign at Christmas (the coin was at once taken and put in a savings bank), until half sovereigns ceased to be minted; and (more important because it was not seized for investment) a shilling whenever we met in Union Street, the main thoroughfare in the city. George's avuncularity was not immediately apparent. He had a plain, if not ugly, face and gingery hair thinning on top. His manner was gruff and, when small children, we were quite frightened of him.

This was the state of things in 1909 and for some time thereafter. In 1912 John married and entered into his inheritance at Goval. Of Papa's two sisters, Kate had died and Maggie acquired for herself a house in Aberdeen and another house for a change of air at Aboyne. In 1914 war came. John, exerting himself too greatly in the absence of the usual manpower, had a stroke and thereafter had to lead the careful life of a semi-invalid. In 1918 Dick was killed in the great spring offensive which was General Ludendorff's last attempt to avert defeat. So Connie was left a childless widow. She was an earnest episcopalian and spent herself and a good deal of her money in the service of the Church and of Jeannie. She sold the house in Rubislaw Den South and bought a smaller one in a less fashionable part. She exchanged the customary menage of cook and housemaid for a single servant, namely, the above mentioned Jeannie, and passed much of the day devising ways of saving Jeannie trouble and making sure she did not overwork. Jeannie revealed herself as a highly skilled recipient of such attentions and became a devoted retainer.

I have left to the last Uncle Theodore, the fourth and youngest of the boys. He had a dismal youth without a mother and with a frightening father who did not, after his wife's death, trouble himself about his children's education. John had been sent to Clifton and George put into the Navy; Theodore went as a day boy to Gordon's College in Aberdeen. Suddenly, with the death of his father he became rich and independent, for Jim, who was his guardian, was a gentle supervisor.

The inheritance of the three older boys had been largely in shares in the business of which they were all directors. But Theodore, like the girls, had his portion in cash, though since he was a male it was not tied up. Once his portion was settled there was no reason why he should not go to Oxford and he did. Jim disapproved of a young man not only doing nothing, but of appearing not to do anything: he must have a profession. So Theodore read for the Bar, was called by Lincoln's Inn and took no further interest in the law. His lifelong interest was in theosophy. He became a disciple of Mrs Besant[1] and for many years served her faithfully in her establishment at Adyar, Madras. He had an enormous admiration for her, especially as an orator. She sounded from his account rather an imperious woman. 'Crombie', she would say sitting at her desk, 'pick up my pen!' and he did so at once.

But he came home often in the hot weather and always to Aberdeen. So the Crombie family, though topographically broken up, was otherwise closely knit. It was an age in which seniority was respected, that is, seniority among males. Uncle Jim, as the eldest brother, was the titular head of the family. Females had no seniority as between themselves. A sister or an aunt earned respect only on matters in which she had made herself the family authority.

In this sphere Janny had the strongest position. On church matters she was able to obtain pronouncements from Lucy's brother, Canon Newill. She had a head for figures and so spoke with authority on household accounts; her dictum that the 'rebate' (all dividends were taxed at the source and the tax on the tax-free portion reclaimed) should be expended on laying in coal for the year, was faithfully followed by my mother throughout her widowhood. Janny and Lucy took an annual holiday in Switzerland, usually at a *pension* in Grindelwald. No one went abroad without consulting them, though it is true to say that the wisdom, while in foreign parts, of inserting emergency cash into the corsets, was initiated by Connie.

Connie was the authority on boys' schools, for she had sent Dick to Uppingham. Grace made the least impact. She murmured through life. She was not a churchgoer, but she was a vegetarian and supported any peaceable type of good cause. She was not as bold as Janny who, though not herself an active suffragette, declared that if Mrs Pankhurst[2] came to her house while on the run (a contingency which never occurred), she would give her shelter. In the important matter of contributions to child welfare, Janny was regular at Christmas and on birthdays in sending postal orders carefully graded from 7/6d downwards according to age, while Grace's good deeds were spasmodic and designed to promote culture. Theodore by contrast never gave anything with any intent but to please the recipient: he once pleased my mother enormously by giving her a pair of

---

[1] Annie Besant, who must then have been about 60, was in the vanguard of female emancipation. Married at 20 to the Vicar of Sibsey, at 26 she left him and her religion and the two children she had borne to him, and formed what the DNB describes as 'a close friendship' with Charles Bradlaugh, the atheist M.P. famous for his refusal to take the oath. She left Bradlaugh and atheism for theosophy, joining the Theosophical Society in 1889 and becoming its President in 1907 and establishing her headquarters at Adyar in 1909. From 1895 onwards India was the scene of her activities, political as well as theosophical. In 1916 she initiated a Home Rule for India League.

[2] Emmeline Pankhurst was the leading suffragette in the first three decades of the century.

hairbrushes with beautifully enamelled backs and handles which she thought too grand to use.

Grace was the authority on wine (though I could not discover any ground for this except a story that she had once got slightly tipsy on mulled claret) with the exception of port. To lay down the law on port was the privilege of those who had inherited the pipe. So Uncle George was the one who 'knew about port'.

Uncle George was undoubtedly the most forceful of the four brothers. He would, I believe, have been an excellent businessman and it was a tragedy for him that the sale of the Grandholm mill left him at a loose end. He had no intellectual interests as had Grace and Theodore, for example. While the mill was still in the family he had a part-time occupation as a director, but after the sale too much of his day was spent in looking for diversions.

Family affairs were his greatest interest. I doubt whether in that sphere ability would have been allowed to oust seniority, but in (the period towards which I am now hurrying,) the period that began with the conversation with my father at Easter 1925, there was no conflict between them. For of his elder brothers, Jim, had died in 1921 and John was inactive with a weak heart. Thereafter George, who rarely left Aberdeen, was unquestionably the family chairman and Connie, who delighted in the use of the telephone, the secretary: the business was the collection and distribution of news about what everybody in the family was doing.

George did not, though a bachelor, need to devote any part of the time left on his hands to his household arrangements. He employed a cook-housekeeper, Mrs Morrison, aided by a kitchenmaid, a tablemaid and a housemaid. Outside there was Duncan who looked after the cars and the garden. Mrs Morrison (the *Mrs* was a courtesy title bestowed in those days on the chief female in the household who was usually a spinster) and Duncan served him for a lifetime; there were only occasional changes among the others.

This was the menage at 64 Rubislaw Den South. In the early 1920s Uncle George bought from Willie Leslie, a cousin who had married a Crombie, Fairgirth, a house at Milltimber with a sizeable garden and a gardener that went with it. Duncan and Grant, the gardener, had cottages and there was enough room in the policies (or the messuages, as the English would call them), for Duncan, now relieved of the horticulture, to keep hens and provide eggs for the house.

Although it was customary to lavish praise on Mrs Morrison's cookery, especially her oatcakes, she was not really a very good cook. This did not matter since Uncle George was not a gourmet; on the contrary he was abstemious and moreover he rarely entertained. I never in twenty-five years met at his house anyone outside the family or heard of any such person ever having been there, and for the family there was only one occasion that could be called a party and that was given in the evening of Christmas Day to eat the customary turkey, plum pudding and mince pies. Then

31

before we reached the port we drank the only other wine in his cellar, *Veuve Clicquot* 1899. It was a fashionable champagne in his youth; a quarter of a century later it was a quiet wine, perhaps no longer what it was meant to be, but very good.

This was the only evening on which he wore a dinner jacket. Usually for dinner he changed out of tweeds into a dark blue suit and wore pumps instead of shoes. Comfort without ostentation; tablemaids rather than butlers and footmen; an ordinary suit for dinner, but an expensive one made by a London tailor; whisky rather than wine. These were the habits of the well-to-do gentry which Uncle George followed. The whisky decanter, usually from a tantalus which he unlocked, was placed on the table beside him together with a tumbler, a port glass and a siphon of soda water. The port glass was there as the measure of the whisky to go into the tumbler. My father followed the same practice but at lunch. Exceptionally Uncle George had at the end of dinner another port glass and a decanter of Sandeman 1890 put on the table.

From what I have written so far you might suppose Uncle George to be a recluse. This was not so. He liked company, but only on his own terms. He had none of the consolations of a recluse which would have enabled him to dispense with it. He never meditated about anything and he did not read much. There were books in a bookcase containing the popular novels, such as Kipling and Rider Haggard of his youth; he did not buy books; he subscribed to *Punch* and to *The Strand Magazine*.

He had not had a liberal education. In the navy somewhere in the Mediterranean he caught a bug and the consequences were serious; he was invalided out and left with a leg of which he had not the full use, a permanent limp and a good deal of pain. He had a good eye in a ball game and so in spite of his handicap played golf well and in his younger days tennis and badminton. He never got rid of the pain and never mentioned it. But it made him easily irritated and sometimes short-tempered, defects fed by his rejection of self-pity and of any outlet that self-pity would have found. He never acquired any taste for discussion. If the subject interested him at all, he would state his opinion and listen unmoved to any opinion to the contrary: argument was excluded.

I have said that he liked company on his own terms. His social life was dominated by the principle that he never put himself out. People must take him as they found him. He would not have called himself hospitable and he would have been right since the essence of hospitality is that the host puts the guest's pleasure first. When Theodore stayed with him, George never altered a regime which left Theodore to shift for himself. It began with breakfast and the newspaper, after which he left home. If the day was fine, he drove to Balgownie and played a round of golf – with a pro unless he came across a congenial member – and lunched at the golf club. If it was wet, he went to the Royal Northern and lunched there. Whether it was the one or the other, he lunched frugally.

So it was golf if fine and bridge if wet. He was an excellent card player and belonged to a small club for duplicate bridge with players of his own standing. After that he might call on us or on Connie or on some other of the connection around teatime to receive a later bulletin of family news. He drove home in time to hear the six o'clock news on the wireless, take a bath, dine and listen to the nine o'clock news. He rarely lunched at home except on Sundays and never dined out.

We were all fond of him and found his 'I say what I think' attitude to life congenial. While he was still at 64 Rubislaw Den South, where it was easy for us to walk across the Den, he would quite often, if he had been with us at teatime and felt like company, invite me to come across for dinner. He had a first class practical mind and his talk on business affairs and money matters was fascinating. I learnt a lot including, rather belatedly, 'the facts of life'.

At the end of our first decade in Aberdeen my father was as far off as ever from making a living as an architect. Half of the decade was wartime and not a good time for an architect struggling to acquire a private practice. When Uncle John moved into Goval he employed my father to reconstruct the interior which he did to very good effect. But as a source of social contacts which might lead to work, the Crombie connection was left untouched. He took a small office in Union Street and waited for the work to come. A club is, among other things, a place where useful contacts may be made. As a Crombie by marriage my father was at once elected to the Royal Northern. But he never went there and my mother came to grudge the annual subscription of seven guineas.

Nor did the Catholic connection provide much of a living. The convent school at Queen's Cross to which we all went as children extended its premises to incorporate the house next door. My father designed the necessary links and also a new chapel. He found the nuns of the Sacred Heart rather unworldly. There lurked in the background of their temporal dealings the notion that the services given to them by the Catholic laity in their pious works should be left unflavoured with commercial considerations. 'You will get your reward in the next world', the Reverend Mother once assured my father when he presented a note of his fees. Monsignor Meany put that right. But any caller at the convent was in peril of being pressed into service. The nuns were unfamiliar with the topography of a city in which they never walked and assumed that it would be simple matter for any resident to deliver by hand a note or letter to any other resident. Fortunately, there was a pillar box just outside the convent gates. But it meant that my father on any visit had to furnish himself with an abundance of penny stamps. There were several French nuns in the community and my father took some of his reward in the form of French lessons.

Outside the city of Aberdeen the rectors of the parishes throughout the diocese exercised a high degree of autonomy. Some, I believe, had life tenure; but the desirability of employing a Catholic architect was a point at which the bishop could, if he wanted, bring pressure to bear. Aeneas Chisholm, Bishop of Aberdeen, was a priest who had served all his life in the diocese. Appointed in his sixties, by 1909 he was in his seventies which meant that by the criteria of the time he was advanced in old age; he left a great deal to his Vicar-General.

But in August 1914 war was declared and for the duration architecture was in decline. In January 1918 Bishop Chisholm died at the age of 82. It was thought certain in the diocese that Monsignor Meany would succeed. Like Bishop Chisholm he had served all his life in the diocese; so if the Church was to provide rewards in this world as well as in the next, he was reasonably sure of the mitre and the crozier. But there was now a fashion for younger bishops and the place was given to a man in his early forties from a large parish in the south of Scotland. Bishop Bennett, coming into office in the last year of the First War, held it until the last year of the Second and Monsignor Meany served under him.

Like the Monsignor the new bishop was a cultivated man of the sort my father liked and which was still quite rare among the Scottish Roman Catholic clergy. The bishop and he were friendly in the rather stilted way in which the Roman Catholic laity of that time related to their bishops.

Meetings began with a genuflection and the kissing of the ring; my father always addressed him as 'My Lord'. They frequently played golf together; the invitation always came from the bishop and was always accepted. The bishop came to tea at our house once in the year on Christmas Day; he was never invited but he always came and it was not to be thought of that any of us should be absent.

But the bishop allowed the diocese as far as possible to run itself. He was not an interventionist. Homilies on the duty to employ a Catholic architect were not his style. The murmurings of the Vicar-General left him unstimulated and there was deep sadness when the theological college at Blairs placed a large piece of architecture elsewhere. Monsignor Meany went so far as to hint to my mother that the bishop was weak. My father would not have dreamt of having even the gentlest word about this with the bishop at the nineteenth hole.

One client came from the Catholic connection. He was Major Malcolm Hay of Seaton who for some reason which I never learnt wanted a house at Clinterty a few miles away. The Hays were members of the congregation and had the pew in front of ours at the Cathedral. They were, I think, descended from the Scottish nobility, though my only evidence for this is, first, that the road to Seaton House was, when the locality had become urbanised, labelled by the municipality Lord John Hay's Road; second, that only a person nobly born could have without embarrassment habitually driven his friends in a very noisy and uncomfortable vehicle called a

Trojan. A. J. A. Symons, the author of that fascinating book *The Quest for Corvo*[1], discovered in the course of the quest that Baron Corvo or Fr. Rolfe – he went under both names – had tutored Malcolm and his brother at Seaton.

My father and Malcolm Hay got on very well together, both having a taste for erudite conversation: Major Hay wrote several books on points in Scottish history. My father liked his unconventionality and lack of ostentation while we liked in particular the eldest daughter Betty.

Meanwhile the cost of living had risen, was rising and was not likely to be diminished. The pound in 1925 had lost half its 1900 value and the rate of income tax had quadrupled. My mother's income was stationary. The trust, the great Victorian device for the protection of money, assumed the impregnability of sterling; when the assumption failed, the trust became and for long endured as one of the chief ways in which wealth was drained from the old, upper and middle classes into the flexible pouches of the new rich, and so it was with my mother's inheritance. There were now five children (my younger brother William was born in Aberdeen in 1911) at school. Somehow my parents paid all the school fees. In all other respects strict economy was necessary. Uncle George gave my mother a cheque for £100 at Christmas and another on her birthday. Sometimes he would offer to pay for a particular project: then an account had to be rendered and items disallowed might be struck out. By a tacit arrangement school fees fell outside the range of benefactions. My parents were adamant about a Catholic education; Uncle George was not a bigot but he was unsympathetic to preferences of this sort.

In this respect the University was different and he paid for me to go to Cambridge in 1923. Although Uncle George could have had no religious objections to the University of Cambridge, I should have thought there would have been other objections even stronger. For my father, no man who had not been to a university could call himself completely educated. For Uncle George, when a boy left school he was old enough to shift for himself. It was a view widely held at the time that, unless a university degree was needed as a qualification, Oxford and Cambridge should be regarded as finishing schools to which parents who could afford the fees could send their sons to learn a little and have a good time.

Undoubtedly my father took the initiative in sending me to Cambridge but the situation was not as simple as that. I shall not go into the complications. I set out to write an introductory chapter to my early days in the law and I have already expanded it into two. It is enough to say that Uncle George agreed to pay all the bills, at first cautiously, a toe in the water to test the temperature, but later with generosity. At the start of my second year he put me on an annual allowance of £300. This had to cover university and college fees as well as maintenance. All the

[1] Cassell (1934) pp. 33 and 55.

same it was a good allowance and as much, I am sure, as he would have given a son of his own. Many at Cambridge had less and few had more.

Two things, I believe, contributed to this happy result. One was my success at the Cambridge Union: I was elected to the Committee at the end of my first year. Papa seems to have instilled into his sons that one of the most important things in business or public life was the ability to stand up and talk firmly and persuasively. The other thing, I suspect but do not know, was the influence of Uncle Theodore. After the war was over and he had moved to Bombay, Theodore came home quite regularly, not every summer but once in two or three. Then he always stayed with George. Even if they went their own ways during the day, they were always together in the evenings.

Theodore had matured into a gentle and sociable bachelor. Life had begun for him at Oxford where, as he told us himself, he was a social success. He enjoyed himself so enormously that he talked about it ever after. It was not done by spending money, of which he had at least four times the average undergraduate allowance. He was proud to relate that at the end of his time one of his friends said to him, 'Crombie, the only time I realized that you had more money than the rest of us was when I noticed that none of your books was secondhand.'

He had many tales too of life in India – of hornets on the hat (it was not a topee – I wonder why) and of snakes in the pan; and talked occasionally (but very little because he had promised my mother not to propagate theosophy) about his life's work. 'I was reading through some old issues of *The Aryan Path*,' he might say, 'when I came across an article that seemed to me one of the best things I had ever read. Everything was put so clearly and convincingly. When I turned over the page I saw that the initials at the end were …my own'. Nothing of this sort was ever said with a conscious attempt to impress and it was always a pleasure to watch him blowing bubbles of pure satisfaction out of his achievements.

But it was to Oxford that his thoughts always returned and some of it may have got through to Uncle George. He may even have indicated that he would be willing to help financially. That would have been enough, for Uncle George was not a man to share control of the purse strings.

Does what I have written make my father sound feckless and Uncle George mean? Neither would be true. Uncle George was mean only in the etymological sense of the word; he measured with care but he was not niggardly. My father was a prudent and cogitating man. Granted his yearning for professional independence and my mother's ability to give it to him, it was natural and reasonable that he should start off as he did. If they had no children, if there had been no war, if the stability of the 19th century had, as expected, continued for ever, his failure to make independently much of a living would not have mattered a lot. But by 1909 when the failure was manifestly total, when there were four children whom he was determined to educate and quite likely more to come (for of course there was no question of family limitation), then when he was still of an age to secure salaried employment, he should, should he not, have put his duty as a breadwinner first? That he failed to do so was not, I am sure, due to excessive optimism: he was no Micawber. But to what defect in his temperament it was due, I never knew him well enough to guess. Whatever it was, it cost him dear.

It did not cost him his dignity. He obtained the fruits of supplication without losing the respect of Uncle George. He was not of course asking for anything that Uncle George could not easily spare. In 1923 Uncle George was already a very rich man in the sense that he had at his command at any moment at least twice as much as he might want to spend. If this be richness, as I think it is, figures are not significant. He was not a man who talked about his money and he would have dealt rudely with even the most tentative enquiries. I remember his horror some years later at the suggestion that a husband should tell his wife what his income was. But he did in the 1940s relent to the extent of telling my wife, to whom he was greatly attached, that if she were his wife he would do so.

When he died in 1946 he was worth nearly half a million sterling, but in a comparison with 1925 there must be taken into account the twenty years of annual surpluses that lie between them. The accumulation was not miserly; it was simply that, although he denied himself nothing that he wanted, his expenditure never matched his income and that he took pleasure both in looking after his investments and in getting value for money.

John Bell of Aberdeen was a well-known dealer in antiques and Uncle George bought Georgian silver from him. If the authentication of a piece was not gilt-edged, he liked to take a discount and run the risk. He enjoyed bargaining but not haggling. He travelled first class in ships and trains and stayed at good hotels but not the most luxurious and certainly not the most fashionable. When in London he stayed first at the Waldorf and then at the Cumberland Hotel. He went to a London tailor but not the very best.

After my father died, it emerged that he had taken out a mortgage on the house for £300. In those days and in those circles, raising a mortgage was almost as bad as selling capital, something that nobody did unless in dire straits. When he heard about it, Uncle George was quite upset: 'He should have come to me,' he said. This made me wonder why so rich a man measured so carefully his outgoings. If he had decided on an annual sum and covenanted to pay it to my parents for seven years, a third or more of it would have been paid out of taxes. That would certainly have appealed to him and then there would have been no uncertainty and no constant reminder of dependence. But it would have been as impossible for Uncle George to do that as it would have been for my father to have made an application for £300. George's generation had been brought up in the tradition of self-help and independence which had been immensely stimulated by the publication in 1859 of Darwin's *Origin of the Species*. The logical consequence of that book was expressed in the phrase coined by the philosopher Herbert Spencer 'the survival of the fittest'. Today this philosophy in a diluted form is called Thatcherism. Under it charity is not condemned, but its dispensation must be carefully supervised. It must never be allowed to interfere with the operation of the proverbial wisdom that a man must cut his coat according to his cloth. This was a matter of principle.

The 'cloth' was what was provided for a man by the enterprise, industry and thrift of himself and his ancestors. Laxity in the observance of the principle would be an erosion of the virtues on which the prosperity of the whole community depended. It was a principle which could easily be impaired by compassion, not merely by public or generalised compassion, which was simply the spending of other people's money, but by private and individual compassion unless it was careful and restrained. Much ingenuity was expended in devising routes along which charity could safely be channelled and in thwarting beggars. Of course human nature being what it is compassion was bound to creep in. Just as pastoral theology devises mitigations of the sterner precepts of the moral theologian, so the needs of the poor might be alleviated by leaks from the tanks of prosperity. But all that sort of thing must be off the record. For the record, the ant was perfectly right to shut the door in the face of the grasshopper.

It was true that for Uncle George the 'cloth' had been provided metaphorically as well as literally by Grandholm Mill. It was the great principle of property that prevented this from making any difference. The assimilation of what was inherited to what was earned by the sweat of the brow was indeed vital to the system. If inheritance was not equated with acquisition the time would surely come when the ant, having stored enough for all the winters she could expect, would be tempted to join in the summer antics of the grasshopper.

So it went against the grain for Uncle George to provide for people who ought either to be providing for themselves or doing without. 'To him that hath…' Uncle George had no qualms about gifts to the self-supporting. He would have given to Theodore anything he wanted if Theodore would have taken it. Moreover, he never thought of what he gave as generosity. He appreciated exactly, though he would not have put it into exact words, the distinction between generosity and liberality. Liberality gives out of abundance: generosity gives when it hurts. Uncle George did not think of himself as generous. He did not expect and would have repelled anything much more than a conventional expression of gratitude. When after I had made good at the Bar people would say to him how much I owed to his generosity, he would repudiate it. 'He made his own way,' he said, 'I did only what a father would have done'.

Uncle George died aged 70 in May 1946. As I was a barrister it was thought proper to nominate me as an executor together with David Cochrane, the family lawyer; the fact that I was an English lawyer while the will would be governed by Scots law of which I knew nothing was not regarded as a deterrent.

Uncle George had been taken seriously ill in the preceding winter. The nature of the illness was never mentioned and I took it to be cancer about which nothing could be done and he had only a limited time to live.

I first knew about it when he called me on the telephone and asked me to come to Aberdeen to discuss "testimentary dispositions". It was not a simple journey. The war had ended in 1945 but the train service had not emerged from wartime conditions. They were still saving fuel and were coping with demobilisation. It was a long night journey without a seat.

When I arrived Uncle George was in bed where he stayed until he died. It appeared that the day before Sir Somebody Something, a local notability, had called to solicit a subscription to some good cause and had been told that Uncle George was too ill to see anyone. Uncle George had never kept open house but after this he insisted on seeing everyone who called.

He wanted first to discuss his funeral. He was to be cremated of course without any funeral service. Although he was interested in religion he had no beliefs. Sometime before, he had told me that he had put a clause in his will that any beneficiary who attended his cremation should automatically forfeit his legacy. I thought that there might be perils in this; an unscrupulous legatee might urge others to go to the funeral of their dear Uncle George and thereby obtain a larger share for himself. So Uncle George, while keeping in his will that the funeral was to be private, abandoned any retaliatory measures. He wanted me to ring up the undertakers to insist that money should not be wasted on an expensive funeral, but fortunately the line was engaged and the matter passed out of his mind.

Talking with David Cochrane I learnt that the estate would be around £400,000 before payment of death duties. In the will which he had made he had provided for fixed sums to go to those in his service but apart from that his bequests had taken the form of shares in the residue. He now wanted to change this and to leave specific sums. I was, he said, now making a good income at the Bar but I would need capital to fall back on: he would leave me £15,000. The same sum would go to my brother, William, who had spent the war in the army and had not yet been demobilised. Apart from a legacy of £20,000 to Aunt Janny, the only one of the four sisters still alive, this was the highest sum. Other relatives were graded lower down to £2,000 to Aunt Letty. The rest would go to charities.

There was no charity in which he was interested and he wanted suggestions about suitable ones. [Sir Somebody Something was obviously going to get his subscription and this led to a thin stream of other callers]. Aunt Janny, who was high Anglican and a devout church-goer, after some hesitation suggested the church she attended, but then had scruples about furthering her own religion at the expense of others. So Roman Catholics were included.

Uncle George gave David Cochrane the names and an amount for each, coupled with some commentary, but whether or not that went into the will I do not know. He gave £500 to Monsignor Patterson to be spent on the church 'which is the ugliest building in Aberdeen'. Another £500 was left to 'the Sisters of Charity who buzz about here like blue-bottles' (David Cochrane wondered if this was sufficient identification but the Mother Superior said that she knew exactly whom he meant).

Then Aunt Janny said that she had always thought it would be a nice surprise to people who had served one in shops to wake up one morning and find that he or she had been left £50 or £100. We pursued this line as far as we could but Uncle George did not do much shopping. There was great relief when David Cochrane, in some perturbation, announced that he had unfortunately underestimated the amount that would be payable in death duties which had just been increased by the socialist Chancellor of the Exchequer. It must have been one of the few occasions on which this news was greeted with relief. Altogether Uncle George had a good deal of fun.

Aunt Johanna, Uncle John's widow, was shocked to see so much money going out of the family. Why did not Uncle George, having benefited all the charities in which he was interested, leave the money in the family? I think it was because he did not really believe in family obligations. True, that was the start of his own fortune and true that he did believe in people helping themselves. True also that he himself was a typical product of unearned increment and that unexpected wealth has done many persons more harm than good. But no man finds it easy to see himself as subject to the common frailties.

Anyway there was left at the end quite a substantial sum which he left to Aunt Johanna to be used for some charitable purpose. She decided that what Uncle George would have liked most would be the provision of secure homes for elderly persons. So she created a trust, of which my wife and Johanna's eldest daughter Merlyn, were trustees, with all that was left over to serve these ends by buying suitable houses to be divided into flats for old persons.

My father was acutely conscious of the fact, which by 1925 there was no disguising, that he was living on his wife's money. Had he been of the nobility he would have seen nothing against that: to marry an heiress was eminently respectable. But for the class immediately below, the merchant or professional class to which he belonged, it was for the husband to support the wife and not vice versa. A situation in which the husband was supported to a material extent by the wife's family could easily become degrading. It is a tribute to my father, one which with the thoughtlessness of youth I never paid, that there was never any question of that. Their relationship, that must at times have been difficult, was based on mutual respect. How my uncle reconciled the respect with his principles or my father the dependence with his pride I do not know. It is to my discredit that I never thought about it. But it is what I meant when I wrote that my father paid heavily for his misjudgement.

Chapter IV

CAMBRIDGE 1923–1925

THERE were not many English universities in 1923, but there was no difficulty in getting into one for a boy. There was at Cambridge an entrance examination called Little-go. I never heard of anybody who took it since it was difficult to leave school without passing an examination which gave exemption from it. It might have been difficult to get at short notice into one of the more fashionable colleges. But I was very content to go to Christ's College which my father had been told would have vacancies for the likes of me. So I was enrolled or matriculated, whatever the correct term was, and went there. I was put down to read History for the first part of the Tripos.

I have said that at school I won half of a prize for debating. The Cambridge Union Debating Society was founded in 1815, some years earlier than its counterpart in Oxford. In 1836 Macaulay sat in the presidential chair. But no other name could be mentioned in 1923 to compare with those which had made the Oxford Union so famous, – Gladstone and Asquith and for a prospective barrister the names of F. E. Smith and John Simon.

As well as an impressive debating hall, the Union provided club premises as comfortable as any in London. My father bought for me for 7½ guineas a life membership and I used it first to go to the opening debate of the Michaelmas Term 1923. This was conducted with ceremony. The President, Vice-President and Secretary, who had dined (incidentally the Union had a remarkably good kitchen) with the speakers whose names were printed on the order paper, entered the hall in procession at 8.15 pm precisely, the officers in white tie and tails and the speakers in black tie and dinner jackets. I remember still the names of the officers I then saw. Putting them in order of precedence, which happens to be the reverse order of their distinction in afterlife, the President, R. H. L. Slater, became a parson. He had stayed on, as was not uncommon, until his fifth year to reach the chair. The Vice-President, a man with dark, bold and handsome looks just falling short of the saturnine, was S. V. or Sam Adams, the son of the incumbent of the Round Church, the historic building which sits beside the Union in successful competition with the latter's Victorian brick. Adams was a colourful personality and an innovator. In his presidency in the following term he introduced birth control as a debatable subject. There was a record attendance at the debate in February 1924 at which the controllers, headed by Lord Dawson of Penn, were victorious by 512 votes to 315.

As Vyvyan Adams he became an unconventional Conservative M.P from 1931-1945 and was tragically drowned in 1951.

The Secretary was R. A. Butler, known to all as Rab, about whom I shall have more to say.

In my first term I made several attempts to speak. Once I was among the 'also spoke' who caught the President's eye at the tail end of the debate which closed at midnight. The man who made his mark with the only speech that gained attention was A. M. Ramsey of Magdalene who, as Bishop of Durham and Archbishop of York and then of Canterbury, became better known as Michael Ramsey.

I went home to Aberdeen for the Christmas vacation of 1923. There were the usual Christmas dances and one of them was at Chanonry Lodge, the residence of the Principal of the University, Sir George Adam Smith. One of his daughters, Janet[1], of the same age as myself, was then at Somerville at Oxford. Ours has been the longest of my friendships, for it began earlier and lasted longer than any other I can think of. She told me she had a cousin at Cambridge, R. A. Butler, who had, she thought, become something at the Union.

Here then was a man who might contrive my ascension from the group of pre-midnight speakers with their two or three minute limits to the middle group who came on after the speakers on the paper had finished and who were given five or ten minutes each. Adams was now President and Butler Vice-President: by convention the election to the Secretaryship was the only one that was fought. Rab was in rooms at Pembroke College. I planned to call on him and introduce myself on a wet afternoon when I might hope to find him in and at an hour when I might be invited to stay to tea. The plan was successful and I did stay to tea. It was the beginning of a friendship which lasted until Rab's death in 1982, as well as of a Union career.

This was in January 1924. I was called early in the next debate and spoke well enough to be put on the paper later in the term in opposition to Ramsey. Although we were of the same year at Cambridge, Michael was a year older than I and that year is the measure of the respectful distance I kept behind him during the whole of our time at Cambridge.

Meanwhile, I was making progress at the Christ's College debating society, named after the college's most prestigious old boy, the Milton. The activists at the Milton were Maurice Perlzweig, David Hardman and my contemporary Leslie Hutchinson. They were all socialist: it was the first time I had met anyone of such a persuasion. Leslie was the mildest of the three. David was the most vigorous: 'Class, class, class,' he would declaim, 'the system is rotten'. After he went down he

---

[1] Janet Adam Smith, author and journalist.

stayed on in Cambridge in local politics, entered the House in 1941 and held junior office in the Attlee government of 1945. Perlzweig was taking a postgraduate course and was five or ten years older than the rest of us. I thought him the most attractive speaker of his time. He was already a rabbi and after his move to New York in 1941 a leading figure in world Jewry.

The meeting with Rab had another consequence of more immediate importance for me. One of Rab's uncles was Sir Geoffrey Butler, a fellow of Corpus and the junior burgess for the University, that is, he was one of the two who represented the University in the House of Commons, one being by convention a don in residence and the other a graduate of distinction in the outside world. Sir Geoffrey was a man of great kindness and geniality and with all the ability, political and academic, of the Butlers. He divided his time between the House, where he was PPS to Sir Samuel Hoare, then Secretary of State for Air (and also, and not entirely by chance, an honorary fellow of Corpus), and Cambridge where he saw himself as recruiting a part of the Conservative elite for the next generation. It was to be an elite of nobility and talent but above all of patriotism, of men who believed in Britain and its future and who would work with all of every class who held a similar belief, an England in which class differences were submerged rather than abolished.

David Hardman had not convinced me of the iniquities of the class system: I thought it at worst a decorative irrelevance, while at best it had a definite appeal for those who today would be described as 'young and upwardly mobile'. While I should always have recoiled as far from the right wing of the right party as from the left wing of the left, fundamentally I believed, then and now, in individualism rather than collectivism. By the time I was put on the paper at the Union with Michael Ramsey I must have become a card-carrying Conservative since the motion, which I supported and he opposed, alleged that the Liberal party was moribund.

Sir Geoffrey, who was of course the President of the University Conservative Association, was very good at getting the younger M.P.s to come down and speak. Before the meeting he always invited the members of the Committee to dine in his rooms at Corpus to meet the speaker. The card that invited us, for it was not long before I became one of the gathering, had 'Black tie', symbolic of the class system, written in the lefthand corner and we always drank champagne. There was an occasion on which Sir Geoffrey substituted an Empire wine but after a few complimentary sips we reverted.

I remember meeting Duff Cooper and Walter Elliot this way. But the man whom I liked best was Stanley Baldwin. Vyvyan Adams, President in the Lent Term of 1924, got him to speak at the Union on one of his non-political subjects,

Rhetoric being the Harlot of the Arts, or something like that, and Sir Geoffrey gave a party for him in his rooms. Of all the great men I met as a young man, Mr Baldwin was with one exception the most impressive because he made no effort to impress. The one exception was not perhaps a true exception because he was more than a great man, he was a magnetic force: Lloyd George could with a look, a handshake or a word lift you off the ground and you could think of nothing else until you came to earth again. But the ordinary great man cares too much about appearing to be great to have thoughts to spare for the person he is talking to. Mr Baldwin seemed to have thoughts for nothing else. Was I thinking of Parliament? How was I going to manage? The Bar had been the way of entry for many successful men. Take F. E. And barristers were always needed. And so on.

F. E. Smith, later Lord Birkenhead, was the man whose career at the Bar every young barrister strove to emulate. Most Presidents of the Oxford and Cambridge Unions tried to get him to speak in a debate and Robert Stevenson succeeded in the summer of 1928. He invited me and Peter (Selwyn) Lloyd[1] to speak on the paper on this occasion. When we dined beforehand and before the specially ordered champagne had begun to flow freely he proved to be rather difficult. An attempt at smalltalk by an unfortunate young man who said he had seen a photograph of him in the Wadham Second XI roused the great man temporarily to a severe rebuke; it was, he said, the First XI. But after the debate was over and the champagne was flowing again he became a good deal more expansive. When he heard that Peter and I were going to the Bar, he told us that we must join Gray's Inn.

This was one of the institutions to which he was intensely loyal. He had indeed done an immense amount for the Inn which up till that time had been the smallest and the least significant. He said that they were very generous with scholarships, etc. and would pay the pupil's fee for anyone whom they thought likely to get on at the Bar; he said just to let him know when I wanted to join.[2]

In the Trinity term Rab was President and put me on the paper at the best of his debates when we had visiting speakers from the United States. The Americans took debating more seriously than we did. Indeed they made it a team sport for which they were trained; they had coaches to keep them up to the mark and to exhort; they had judges who awarded points and declared the winners. Rab, who arranged the debate at Cambridge, gracefully acknowledged the American practice by inviting two of our American dons to act as judges. About one of them, Arthur Goodhart, I shall have much more to say.

[1] See page 68.

[2] Actually he there and then promised a £100 scholarship which offer, when the time came, he had forgotten. He eventually honoured the promise.

The other, G. T. Lapsley, was then in his early fifties. He had been a fellow of Trinity for the past twenty years having graduated at Harvard in 1893. His speciality was mediaeval English constitutional history and he was an acknowledged authority on what went on in the County Palatine of Durham. At this time he and D. A.Winstanley were the two college tutors. He became so deeply absorbed in the ethos of the higher social life of Trinity as to provoke Winstanley's *mot* that if in some corner of England Lapsley were to die, he would wish to be buried simply as The Unknown Etonian.

He was a strong anti-feminist, practising what he preached in a life of excessive celibacy. He talked in the same way as he lectured, drily and wittily with precision laced with pedantry. His lectures were given in the hall of Trinity and attracted a large and appreciative audience. Law students went because he made mediaeval land law interesting. There were usually some girls from Girton, sent there perhaps by Helen Camm, the Girton historian, said to be one of the two women whom he tolerated. (The other was Edith Wharton; he was her literary executor; they were both admirers of Henry James and belonged to the coterie at Rye). But the girls were segregated on the east wall as much as possible out of sight. He always addressed his audience as 'Gentlemen'.

It would be off-hand to call him a snob. He was a connoisseur and collector of those whom he classified – these were his very words to Jack Hamson, one of his Trinity pupils – as well-born, as goodlooking and as intelligent in that descending order of merit. It sounds odd, but I dare say that it is only reflecting an older fashion. Forty years before this Trollope put his requisites for a statesman as rank, intellect and parliamentary habits: only the last is now thought necessary.[1]

I sat next to Mr Lapsley[2] at the dinner before the debate and it is possible that I scraped into his third class, for when President of the Union I was invited to one of his formal parties in his rooms in Neville's Court where, as his obituary in *The Times* says, 'he excelled in literary allusion and repartee'. He was a Cambridge 'character' commemorated only in an uncommunicative brass memorial to him in Trinity College chapel. Its inadequacy has tempted me into these paragraphs. But really all that I have to say about him in my present context is that he and Arthur Goodhart discharged their judicial duties admirably with judgments so oracular that it was impossible to say who had won. The debate had the largest audience of the term; thanks to this I was elected to the Union Committee at the end of my first year, the only one of that year to achieve the honour.

The centre-piece of the Michaelmas term which started my second year was the general election of 1924 at which the first Labour government fell and Mr Baldwin

[1] Anthony Trollope, *An Autobiography*, Oxford University Press (1923) p. 328.

[2] 23 August 1949. There is a 'spoof' interview with him (probably by Romney Sedgwick) in the *Trinity Magazine* November 1921. I am indebted to Professor C. J. Hamson of Trinity College for much of this information.

was returned to power. Cambridge town was well supplied with workers for the cause; in the county and in the adjoining constituency for the Isle of Ely undergraduates were needed to keep village meetings going until the candidate arrived. Dick Briscoe was the successful candidate for the county and Hugh Lucas-Tooth in the Isle of Ely. They were not ships that I passed in the night. In the 1930s my wife and I had a weekend cottage in Cambridgeshire, a mile away from Dick's estate at Longstowe, and got to know him very well; and in the 1950s Michael Oppenheimer [1], my wife's nephew, married one of Hugh's daughters, Helen.

I was now one of three hopefuls on whom Sir Geoffrey kept an eye. His nephew Rab was of course the first; for him the uncle foresaw a fellowship at Corpus and a university seat. The second was Geoffrey Lloyd, a great friend of Rab, who had been elected Secretary of the Union at the end of the Lent term 1924. Sir Geoffrey was the godfather of all our careers and the other Geoffrey was one of the first of his recruits, in his case one might almost say 'converts'. For Geoffrey Lloyd when he first came up to Trinity from Harrow, was (so I was told, for he was three years senior to me) interested in term time only in hunting, drinking and punting on the Cam, preferably naked in inconspicuous stretches; and during vacations interested chiefly in the pleasures of Parisian life. He was a member of the Cambridge Athenaeum, which was not an offshoot of the London club but the peer of the Oxford Bullingdon. He had private means of the widow's cruse type, inexhaustible rather than enormous: he did not surround himself with riches but supplies of what he wanted never faltered. When I first got to know him properly, he had rooms in St John's Street, a large sitting room which when evening came was lit only by candles. I liked having tea there on a winter evening; tea, toast and Gentleman's Relish, never any variation. He was astounded by my ignorance of life. Several times he said that I must meet those whom he described without particularising as 'my friends'. It never happened, so he must have thought it too experimental. To those whom he liked he was a very good friend indeed.

Sir Geoffrey got him interested in politics and active not only in the Conservative Association but in the Union, the latter not being a place frequented by his friends. Indeed he became almost too much of a politician. At Cambridge we thought that he would go further than Rab. Was not Rab, who busied himself about getting a double first, too academic? (Rab's father seems to have shared our view; he advised Rab to set his sights on the Speaker's chair[2]). But though Geoffrey was for many years the 'boss' of Birmingham Conservatives, held several second-class ministries and distinguished himself particularly by his work on Pluto (pipe line under the ocean) which fed the great invasion of 1944, his career is not to be compared with Rab's.

---

[1] Sir Michael Oppenheimer, expert on Italian historic buildings, and Lady Oppenheimer is a well known Theologian.

[2] Lord Butler, *The Art of the Possible*, Hamish Hamilton, p. 21.

For me it was obvious that I could not go into politics without an income; the salary of an M.P. was £400. I had no inclination to a life in commerce and no aptitude for it.

The Bar was certainly the profession most easily combined with politics. I suppose that during the vacation of 1924 I gave some sort of hospitality to these thoughts but they were the concern of a world that was still remote.

In the autumn teams set out from Oxford and Cambridge to challenge American universities in the East and the Middle West; those of the Far West were, when travel was by boat and train, too far away to be reached within a limited timetable. Rab was one of the Cambridge team and in the States for much of the Michaelmas term of 1924.

The main event of the next term was the Annual Dinner early in March of the University Conservative Association. Geoffrey Lloyd was the Secretary of the Association. But he was also in that term the President of the Union and he delegated to me much of the work of organising the dinner. It was held at the Lion in Petty Cury. I was a member of the select body which met in the early afternoon to approve the menu and choose the wines. The bill of fare had not an appealing look and Rab improved its appearance by turning it into French. His rendering of Winchester Cutlet as *Cotelette Rissolée à la Wykeham* struck the higher note. We sipped the main wine, followed Sir Geoffrey in his mouthings and echoed his opinion that it had not much body but that anything better would strain the budget.

The guest of honour was the Marquess Curzon of Kedleston, the 'superior purzon' of anecdote, a great servant of Empire, Sir Geoffrey said, whom the young should learn to appreciate at his true worth. It was not quite two years since, as Curzon wrote, 'the cup of honourable ambition had been dashed from my lips'.[1] This was when he received the news that the insignificant Mr Baldwin had been preferred to him as Prime Minister. He was now about to face death with the like astonishment that he could be treated in such a way. He was spending the night at the Master's Lodge at Christ's (Sir Arthur Shipley enjoyed the reception of distinguished guests) and dressing for the dinner when he was seized by the recurrence of a pain which he had dismissed as a passing indisposition. A surgeon was sent for, an operation decided upon and Lady Curzon arrived to take him away. He assured the Prime Minister that he would get through the operation but a fortnight later he died.

Meanwhile the dinner had been eaten in his lamented absence. Fortunately the Senior Burgess, the Right Honourable J. F. P. Rawlinson, was present. He was a

[1] Ronaldshay, Earl of. *The Life of Lord Curzon*, Vol. 3, p. 352. London, Ernest Benn, 1928.

K.C. used to such emergencies and he made an emergency speech. It was a minor consequence of the tragedy that I was never able to say that I had watched Lord Curzon consuming a Winchester Cutlet at the Lion Hotel. Instead I was the recipient of one of those acts of courtesy which he was generally supposed to withhold from his inferiors. At Sir Geoffrey's suggestion I called at the Lodge the next morning to leave on behalf of the undergraduate company a note of sympathy and regret. The Master told me that he insisted on sitting up in bed to pencil two paragraphs in reply. Of course I have lost the reply.

It must have been about this time that the Cambridge team to tour the Middle West in the fall of 1925 was being selected. The tour would begin in mid September and finish towards the end of November, leaving less than a fortnight of the Michaelmas term. Geoffrey Lloyd, who was just finishing his term as President, was an obvious choice to lead the team. David Hardman would be President in the Michaelmas term, triumphantly the first Socialist to hold the office. Certainly he was the first active Socialist, though it was rumoured that Slater held to some type of ecclesiastical socialism. Obviously the President could not go to the States. Michael Ramsey, who would be Vice-President, would take his place. The third place was offered to me.

These were the matters that prefaced my conversation with my father at Easter 1925 when I made my choice of the Bar. It was a choice that called for a fourth year at the university. The Cambridge Tripos is in two parts, the first being completed in two years and the second usually in the third year. Having read history in the first part, it was thought hazardous for me to attempt a new subject in a single year and impossible if that year was virtually reduced to two terms.

Would Uncle George agree to a fourth year? He did agree. Representing Cambridge in America was something tangible (if one takes the wider dictionary definition of 'clearly intelligible, not elusive or visionary') and he dealt in tangibilities. I suppose that by implication he accepted also my idea of going to the Bar though I do not know that he committed himself. One of the unexpectedly nice things about him was the delicacy of his contact with paternal dignity. I was never told what my father and he said to each other; there were never any joint communiqués. Until the end of my days at Cambridge everything was conveyed to me as my father's decision.

The Trinity term of 1925 passed uneventfully. It rained a lot. A small group including Rab and myself rented a grass tennis court somewhere by the river near where the Garden House Hotel now is with the idea of playing gently in Arcady; it rained so often that the court was never fit for play when we wanted it.

At the end of the term I stood for the Secretaryship of the Union. It was one of the rare occasions on which a non-party man was elected. A tie on the first count introduced a touch of excitement; on the second with the transferable vote my opponent was victorious. But I could stand again in December since I would be up for a fourth year anyway. I could get back from the States just in time for the seventh debate in the term, the one that immediately preceded the election, and David said that he would put me on the paper with a suitable subject. Rab said that I could leave my interests in his hands.

I went home at the beginning of June with a load of law books to read. These came from David who had just taken the Law Tripos and had no thought of embarking on a legal career. Like Uncle Theodore but not, I expect, so well endowed, he had bought his text books new and generously offered them to me at half price. I began my reading with Salmond on Jurisprudence and enjoyed it enormously. It gave me the thrill, the taste of life in a lucid and well ordered world, that I had first enjoyed at the age of eight when I opened a Latin grammar. The same thrill, I believe, can be found in harmony and in chess. But these are spheres I have not penetrated.

I parted from Rab in Cambridge not expecting to see him again until I got back from America. But at the end of June he wrote from the Ben Wyvis Hotel at Strathpeffer Spa inviting me to stay there. He said that he had been ordered to take the waters of the spa in a most stringent cure and with plenty of exercise. Sir Montagu and Lady Butler were on home leave[1]; she was with Rab at the spa but had to leave at the end of June while the cure did not finish till 7 July. I was delighted with the invitation. I still remember the journey since it was in the days before travel by road was common. To get from Aberdeen to Strathpeffer took the better part of a day. First an 8.00 am train to Inverness: a very lengthy pause there for lunch and a connection: then a journey of an hour and a half with a change at Dingwall and you got to Strathpeffer at teatime. There was, as usual with Rab, a period of acclimatization. But after that, whether in good or bad health, he was always delightful company, light-hearted but with sombre intervals for pondering the verities. There was trawling on the loch, some tennis and long walks. But only the last was permitted on Sunday.

Travel to New York required a visa which was not obtainable in Aberdeen, the nearest American consul being at Dundee. Fortunately a Cambridge friend, Jimmy Prain, had his home at St Andrews and I spent an agreeable couple of days there while his father, who knew the consul, procured the visa with the added bonus of a letter to the effect that I had been recommended to him (the consul) by a 'substantial citizen'. We sailed to New York on the *Laconia*, a one-class boat that took seven days. There was a parliamentary delegation with wives and daughters going out at the same time. I saw quite a bit of Bob Boothby who had in the 1924

[1] Sir Montagu Butler was Governor of the Central Provinces, 1925-33.

election been returned as the Conservative member for East Aberdeenshire. He was already one of the future prime ministers whose future had attracted Aunt Letty, who claimed to be on familiar terms, but his future was to be unfulfilled. He was interesting on political life.

I saw very little on the voyage of Geoffrey and Michael. We were given three or four days in New York before we started on our schedule of universities. The United States, as everyone knows, is parcelled into three large areas: the East, the Middle West and the Far West. The Far West was treated as 'out of bounds' because it was so distant. The East and the Middle West were taken by Oxford one year and Cambridge the other; there were, in 1925, virtually no other universities which the Americans had heard of. This year it was our turn to take the Middle West. So, we left New York for Detroit which was, so to speak, our opening night. After that we did all the large universities and some of the small ones in the Middle West. Quite a number of them we did from the Drake Hotel by the lake in Chicago.

I found the Americans we met rough and unmannered. They were surly when accosted in the street and on the train they clustered round cuspidors (spitoons) in observation cars. When I next went to the States, in 1947, I was struck by the enormous difference.

In the States, debating is, or was then, taken very seriously indeed. A debate was a contest which had to be trained for and won. Coaches sat behind the teams working a card index system. Whenever a point was raised which was outside their prepared speeches, the coach would pull out a card which contained the answer. Judges awarded points as in boxing and the side with the most points won. This was not the Oxford or Cambridge style where some measure of frivolity was not condemned.

The Americans were not unprepared for this. Of the three subjects selected for debate one was on the virtues of prohibition which at that time was the law in the United States. The other serious subject was the League of Nations which America had opted out of five years before. The third subject was perhaps intended to introduce a lighter touch; the motion was that 'This House pities its grandchildren'?

As the word was carried forward that we were behaving rather flippantly, the Americans became more relaxed, finding that the large audiences enjoyed our silly but spontaneous jokes. I remember that when one American speaker in the prohibition debate said that our speeches had left them in the dark, I said that it was better than being left under the moonshine. When, in another prohibition debate, Geoffrey was confronted with spitting as an example of something that every nation prohibited or restrained, he replied that spitting and drinking were activities in the opposite directions. No doubt this sort of ribaldry was new to American audiences but they seemed to like it while the judges, I dare say, awarded several penalty points.

At one very young and small college, it was announced before the debate began that there would be no judges. This was in deference to the English system in which, they said, the result was decided by votes. When the speeches were over our hosts considerately removed us to a room where we were refreshed with orange juice and barley water. In our hotel the next morning we read in the local newspaper the headline: "Seven year old university defeats seven hundred year old university by three hundred votes to three."

It must have been some time after the middle of November when Michael and I started our return journey. We had had very little contact with the old world: there was no transatlantic telephone; letters took six or seven days and we were always moving about. In October I had had a letter from Rab to say that he had been elected to a fellowship at Corpus and proposing a dinner in his rooms there on my return. This had been timed so that I could speak on the paper in the last debate of the term which was held in early December. Michael and I shared a cabin in the *Mauretania* which rattled her way across in five days. Geoffrey, who had finished with Cambridge stayed behind to explore the Far West.

At the Union election which followed, I was voted into the Secretaryship. On the surface this was the result of a single speech, the only speech of mine which a third of the audience who were freshmen could have heard. I think it would be truer to say that my absence accomplished what my presence at the two previous elections had failed to secure.

Chapter V

CAMBRIDGE 1926–1927

CHRIST'S College is not one of the largest. Its population, as of nearly all the others, overflowed its boundaries and spilt into the laps of surrounding landladies. In my first two years I lived in small and doleful rooms in Earl Street in the purlieus of Parker's Piece. Evenings were isolated since no one except an accredited inhabitant could enter the house after ten o'clock. There was no bath of course; the landlady's daughter brought hot water in a jug when she deemed it to be necessary. There was within the curtilage of the college an old-fashioned bathhouse. I remember walking to it in the winter and in the hardihood of youth across Christ's Piece in dressing gown, pyjamas and bedroom slippers and sometimes in snow and rain. In the States I had observed more up-to-date premises called ablution blocks.

In my third year I was given rooms in college and took possession of them immediately on my return from the States. They were on the ground floor in the First Court and in the far left hand corner of it as you come through the main gate. Not quite at the corner; for the entrance to the chapel is at the right angle which the west wall of the court makes with its north wall which is also the south wall of the Master's Lodge and the Hall.

What makes Cambridge, taken to the last extremities of comparison, lovelier than Oxford is not the architecture which in each place is incomparable. Nor is it the Cambridge showpiece which is The Backs. It is the fact that Cambridge colleges have courts and Oxford colleges have quads. The centrepiece of the court is the lawn, the quad is just a quadrangular floor of a quadrangle. The beauty of the court lies in the opposition to the grass floor of the surrounding walls of brick or stone and fenestration.

The beauty of The Backs lies in the same contrast between grass and stone lifted with the aid of greater space into sublimity. The river adds something because it is sluggish. A fast flowing river would be an intrusion. But the Cam is slow; with lawns coming down to the edge on one side and willows trailing on the other, it does not interrupt; the bridges, Clare's being the most beautiful, are links that do not distract. So you can see at your own level the colleges in their groups with the splendour of King's at the centre; there need be no craning of the neck from the opposite pavement of a traffic-laden street.

Christ's is not one of the river colleges. Its beauty is its own entirely. The first court, wherever it might be put, is lovely. Put it into slums, it would still be lovely.

I do not think that it could be made lovelier by putting it into space. It is an interior loveliness. There is a price to be paid for space: the lack of enclosure means the loss of the interior.

The college is at the centre of the town in one of its busiest parts where in my time four roads met; Petty Cury was not then for pedestrians only. It is unharmed by the bustle and the traffic. Again, it is the contrast that enhances. To cross the threshold at the main gate, maybe, if the heavy gate is shut, to pass through the narrow wicket that lets in only one at a time, to walk by the thickness of the porter's lodge and then to turn right or left along the stone path that surrounds the lawn, is to move out of the snarls of the town into an enclosure that is not quite finite. At the far right hand corner there is an opening through which you can, if you want, pass on your left the doors into the hall and on your right the screens and walk into the second and third courts; then either straight on to the Fellows' Garden or round to the left, past the walled garden of the Master's Lodge to the house fronting on King Street where Arthur Brown[1] lived and dispensed his claret. I said 'if you wanted'. You could also stop in the First Court, saying as one says in a few places in the world, 'This is a place where I shall live and work'.

I lived and worked there for a year and a half. The windows of my sitting-room exposed the First Court. The room was well-proportioned and pleasing, panelled and painted white. It was large enough for a small dinner party; a dining table for six still left space for a sofa and armchairs, a bookcase and a desk. In those days one could have any meal one liked from the college buttery. Breakfast came on a tray, lunch or dinner with a college waiter, wine from the college cellar. I began to learn a little about wine. Once Sir Geoffrey came to dinner – a black tie although we dined alone, but 'black tie' was the formula then not for dressing up but for dressing down from the tailcoat and white tie that was still the dress for a party - perhaps to discuss some aspect of my future or perhaps as some sort of return for all the hospitality he gave. I had ordered a bottle of *Cos d'Estournel* 1906 and was pleased when he approved. The room is still there, much as it was so it seems. But as I pass it now, it looks perhaps upgraded, if not for a Fellow, at least for some species higher than the common undergraduate.

The common undergraduate today exchanges the pleasures that I enjoyed for the conveniences that I lacked. Behind the sitting-room there was a bedroom, the size and shape of a dungeon with a small window admitting some light from King Street, bitterly cold in winter. It created an illusion of life within the walls of a castle keep. There was no bathroom, of course, but the walk to the 'ablution block' was mercifully short.

[1] C. P. Snow's *'The Masters'* (see next page)

The responsibility for education at Cambridge was divided between the University and the colleges. Learning was imparted through the mouths of the tutor and the supervisor provided by the college and of the lecturers provided by the university. The same person might discharge the three functions, being tutor to one pupil, supervising him and others and lecturing to all. The tutor cared for the conduct and welfare of the pupil; the supervisor directed his studies, telling him what lectures to go to and what books to read.

Sidney Grose was my tutor. Christ's has today about a hundred fellows. Sixty years ago it had about twenty of whom about a dozen were active in the life of the college. The reader who wants to know more about the actual fellowship of the college at that time should turn to C. P. Snow's novels, especially *The Masters*.[1] Since his death in 1980 his novels seem to have sunk with the speed of a Trollope. Trollope rose again and Charles will do likewise. No one who can write well and who can depict character and period goes into oblivion; he lives on somewhere whether in literature or in history or in both. The 'Arthur Brown' of the Snow novels is a lifelike and precise drawing of Grose; being a kindly portrait as well as a true one, the accuracy is not disputed.

Grose was the exemplar of the reasonable man, travelling through life on whatever is the Cambridge equivalent of the Clapham omnibus. He was also an agreeable man, though I think that the Arthur Brown qualities were more in evidence with his fellows than with his pupils. When I was President of the Union he gated me for a week because I had been out of college after ten o'clock for more than four evenings in the previous week. I do not think that Arthur Brown would have done that; I doubt if his claret parties ever finished at ten o'clock. A few years ago I came across a card from him, unaccountably preserved. It said that if I did not conquer my bad habit of unpunctuality, it would be a handicap to me in life. When I read it again after an interval of half a century I was shocked. If there is one thing on which I have prided myself it is punctuality. I have only once in my life missed a train and that was my daughter's fault at the Gare du Nord. I now find myself compelled to believe that my punctuality is not innate but the fruit of a well-timed rebuke.

Grose lived to a great old age. After I went down I saw him again only twice. Once when he was approaching the main gate of the college, moving into it ahead of me with a purposeful stride, his mortarboard firmly at right angles to his head and his gown flowing in the rush of air; he was on his way, I did not doubt, from one committee to another, too busy to be stopped. I did not see him again until many years later when I was High Steward of the University and he had become

---

[1] Macmillan, 1951. Charles was a fellow of Christ's in the thirties. But he did not write only about what he knew at first-hand. He was never a lawyer; but his descriptions in his sequence *Strangers and Brothers* of the humbler practice of the law is so realistic that I could hardly believe it to come from imagination and not experience.

identified as Arthur Brown. He was seated on a sofa at a reception at the Fitzwilliam looking not old although he must have been in his nineties, but uninterested in the world and just benign, his round and tranquil face as composed as a Buddha. I wanted to tell him that I had profited by what he had said on punctuality. But he had no idea who I was and to fan embers of memory until they faintly glowed would have put him to trouble with no reward to himself.

But to an undergraduate it was not the tutor that mattered, nor was it the lecturers. They were to be had for the trouble of attendance, some of them at the distasteful hour of 9.00 am. Except for the few personalities, such as Arnold McNair, it was more profitable to get the material out of a book and then to talk about it with the supervisor. It was before the day when the seminar had come to combine and vitalise the lecture and the tutorial.

It was the supervisors who mattered. Mine were numerous and unco-ordinated. Grose was a classical scholar and Christ's had no law don among its fellows until 1951. Sir Geoffrey was aware of this. When I got back from the States I found awaiting me a note from him to say that I should be receiving from Arthur Goodhart an invitation to the luncheon that he gave annually on Thanksgiving Day to Americans in Cambridge; I should be asked to reply for the guests and it was very important that I should accept.

This was the Arthur Goodhart who had been one of the two American judges at the Union debate with the American team at the end of my first year. He was then in his early thirties and at the beginning of a career which he ended half a century later as one of the two best known academic lawyers of his time. I mention two advisedly. It was Arthur who later recommended me always to write 'one of the two' because then, as he said, anyone who thought that he had as good a claim as the name mentioned was left free to think that he was the other one not identified.

Arthur was then one of the younger fellows of Corpus. He was an American of a wealthy New York family; an uncle, a leading Democrat, was one of the senators for the State of New York. After reading law at Yale Arthur came to Cambridge and, though retaining his American nationality and often revisiting, made his home in England.[1]

He was as ugly as he was good and as generous and as witty as he was learned. He was at this time editing the *Cambridge Law Journal* and about to succeed Sir Frederick Pollock (of Pollock on Contract, Pollock on Torts and The Pollock-Holmes letters) in a memorable editorship of *The Law Quarterly Review*. He was devoted to Sir Frederick and endeavoured to acquaint him with the thoughts of the

---

[1] His three sons have all achieved distinction in England. The eldest, Sir Philip, has been a Conservative member of Parliament since 1957; the second, William, a Chancery silk, was a force in the Social Democratic Party; the third, Charles, a prize fellow of Trinity, is a monetary economist who has been an adviser to the Bank of England since 1969.

younger generation; but since Sir Frederick was deaf as well as uninterested, the attempt failed.

As a fellow of Corpus Arthur was made a willing contributor to Sir Geoffrey's good works. He was a lecturer in jurisprudence, but his means made it unnecessary for him to take pupils in whom he was not interested. Sir Geoffrey persuaded him to take in joint session Mervyn Clive[1] and myself.

This set me on the right road for the second part of the law tripos. But my immediate interests were the University Conservative Association, of which I was Secretary, with the immediate duty of organizing the annual dinner, and the Union. In this sphere there had been for me a transformation. Just after Christmas while I was still in Aberdeen I got a letter from Rab to say that he would announce his engagement to Sydney Courtauld soon after the beginning of term: 'I feel happy and sure of the course.'

Sydney had just taken her degree. She had been a force at Newnham as president of the college Conservative Association as well as of the debating society and I had just met her in both capacities. It was not the custom at Cambridge University in those days for male and female society to mix and I had never met her with Rab. Indeed, the attachment had been formed since I had last seen Rab. After he left Strathpeffer Sydney had invited him to stay with her parents and herself on holiday in Norway; in the five months that had passed since then they had seen a lot of each other and the engagement had matured.

It meant certainly a change of course for Rab and a swifter voyage. With his fellowship and the lecturing and teaching which he had already begun he had a comfortable bachelor living. But Sydney was an heiress, the only child of Sam Courtauld the chairman of the company. He could now, if he chose, move straight into political life; the Courtauld influence in East Anglia would secure for him quite quickly a safe seat.

Sydney was uninterested in fashionable life. They planned a quiet wedding after Easter. Rab would give up his fellowship at the end of the academic year. They would rent a house in Cambridge for the Trinity term. They selected a modest establishment called The Gerrans; they were not there long enough to discover what a gerran was. Then they planned a world tour, mostly imperial, as an education for the political world.

But Rab's health had not got back to normal. The Courtaulds took the matter in hand and sent him to see Sir John Atkins, a physician of repute. Sir John strongly encouraged the imperial tour. He thought that a complete change of life seasoned by sea voyages would be just the thing: certainly either that or the course of nature did cure Rab. Meanwhile it was thought that between the end of the Lent term and

[1] Son of the Earl of Powis, descendant of Clive of India. He was killed in the Second World War.

the wedding Rab ought to spend a quiet week in the country. There was a little inn he was fond of Dartmoor where he had once spent a holiday with Willy Wolfson, the closest of his Cambridge friends. He invited me to spend the week with him. Sydney approved of this, but I dare say she wanted to see what I was like. She invited me to lunch at her flat in Vicarage Gate, Kensington. We took a liking to each other at once.

Sydney had a very strong character which she did not conceal. She was forthright in speech and action. Lady Longford in her memoirs[1] recalls as a young girl at the seaside being driven from the water's edge into the sea with the admonition not to be a coward: it sounds not untypical. She was and remained deeply in love with Rab and he, though not a passionate man, was very happy with her. At times her outspokenness must have made difficulties for him. It was an unfortunate irrelevance that she was rich and he was not, since her assertiveness was quite wrongly put down to the possession of the money bags. Sam Courtauld, who sounds a very wise man, saw to it that Rab was not financially dependent. In the end he even made him rich. For he left to Rab an estate in Gloucestershire where the couple never lived; it was the one bought by the Queen as a home for Princess Anne after her marriage to Captain Phillips. On marriage he gave Rab an allowance of £5,000 a year.

As soon as term ended Rab and I went to the Manor Hotel at Dousland where we spent a happy week walking on Dartmoor. The last event of the term was the Conservative dinner which took place at the Lion Hotel as usual. The guest of honour was Winston Churchill, Mr Baldwin's surprise choice in 1924 as Chancellor of the Exchequer. Sir Geoffrey presided with Mr Churchill on his right and myself on Mr Churchill's right. Sir Geoffrey was to make the introductory speech; then I was to propose the health of the guest of honour; then he was to reply with the speech of the evening. Winston in his life of his father had recorded the message of support and sympathy sent to Lord Randolph by the Cambridge Carlton Club (as the University Association was then called) at the time of his fatal resignation. Winston, Sir Geoffrey thought, might like to be reminded of that and with his usual generosity he gave the reminder to me. That was for my speech. Conversation would be more difficult, Sir Geoffrey advised. It was necessary to get Winston going on a subject which he would expand. He was usually ready to talk about Lord Randolph, Sir Geoffrey told me, and of the dramatic finish to his career when 'he forgot Goschen'.

This idea did not meet with the success which it deserved. Naturally Winston talked to Sir Geoffrey most of the time and I had to wait for a suitable moment to tender my contribution. Anxious to give him the broadest latitude for his reply I

[1] Elizabeth Longford, *The Pebbled Shore*, George Weidenfeld & Nicolson (1986) p. 41.

asked him how he thought it ('it' being Lord Randolph's rise and fall) had all come about. He raised his fork slowly and held it in the air pondering. Then he said, 'Events'. He paused. He raised the fork higher and, lifting his voice as if in response to a conductor's baton, he said again 'Events'. Then he replaced the fork and upon a note of finality said, 'Events'.

The matter was not carried further. But in his speech, which was of Churchillian magnificence and could be read in three columns of the *Cambridge Daily News* he elaborated on the incident. The other speeches went well and Mr Churchill noted on the back of his menu card one or two phrases from mine. He left the card on the table and I picked it up and took it with me. But inevitably I have lost it.

The Trinity term was devastated by the General Strike which lasted from 3 May for ten days. There was a general rush to drive trains or buses or to keep the country going in some way or another. Civil commissioners were appointed. Sir Philip Sassoon, who was Under-Secretary for Air, was allocated to East Anglia and Geoffrey Lloyd acted as chief of a staff on which Mervyn Clive and I were given lowly positions; we shared a room from which we dispensed encouragement by telephone to the mayors of the province. The Vice-President of the Union, which was my office in this term, was responsible for the house premises. We set up a news service in the debating hall and made other adaptations to meet the crisis.

But all the heavy work of that sort was done by Stanley Brown, a man of unparalleled efficiency who had been Chief Clerk since 1903 and was to remain so until 1943. He had a distinguished appearance. With a military bearing and a perfectly groomed moustache he looked like a retired colonel from one of the very best regiments who had adapted himself easefully to civilian life. He treated with deference the rapid succession of undergraduate officers who passed through his hands, but his 'Leave it to me, Mr President' was rarely resisted. He was in the happy position of an eminent civil servant whose ministerial boss is changed three times a year. Michael Ramsey surprised me by detaching himself from the national effort. It raised an issue on which the Liberals were divided: was the unconstitutionality of an attempt to dominate society by industrial power to be condoned by its object of achieving social justice? Michael, I think, put the object first. The occasion gave me my first indication that he was more interested in social than political issues. But the indication was not strong enough to counter my surprise when I heard the next year that he was going into the Church.

The social issue was a very real one and had been bubbling for some time. By any neutral standard of value for money the miners were giving more than they were getting, but the owners said that they could afford no increase in wages. On 28 July 1925 the Prime Minister had set up a Cabinet committee under Mr Churchill to find a solution. Within forty-eight hours the committee recommended the appointment of an expert committee to advise on the reorganization of the industry; meanwhile the Government should bridge by a subsidy, the gap between the wage demanded and what was being paid. The proposal was accepted at a Cabinet meeting on 20 July at which the Cabinet Secretary noted 'a strong feeling that the miners have a certain amount of right on their side'.[1]

On 10 March 1926 the Samuel Commission published its report. Like so many other excellent reports it pleased neither side. This would not be surprising if Lord Birkenhead was right in his view that he would have thought the miners' leaders the stupidest men in England if he had not met the owners.[2]

But both sides had to accept that the subsidy would end: the owners declared that the consequence would be an immediate reduction in the wage. Attempts to compromise broke down because the owners would negotiate only local settlements with the wage dependent on what each district could afford while the miners insisted on a national minimum. On 1 May the owners announced the wage reduction, the miners rejected it and the lock-out began. On the same day the T.U.C. Council gave notice of a general strike in support of the miners to commence on 3 May. After little more than a week the General Strike collapsed but the lock-out continued for another six months after which the miners were driven by penury back to work.

The General Strike was a challenge to the sovereignty of Parliament of a magnitude last encountered in the reign of George III. The strike was made practicable, and arguably legal, by the Trade Disputes Act 1906 which had granted immunities to trade unions that placed them above the law; its effect upon jurisprudence as well as upon industrial relations started one of the great debates of the twentieth century.

I had begun to think about the subjects which I should prescribe for debates during my presidency of the Union. Trade unionism struck me as one of profound as well as topical interest. I recalled the motion which John Dunning, a lawyer, had moved in the Commons in 1780: 'that the influence of the Crown has increased, is increasing and ought to be diminished'. I decided upon an echo: 'that the power of Trade Unionism in England has increased, is increasing and ought to be diminished'.

For the first debate of the term it was usual to have six speakers on the paper, two of them leading Union orators, and four public figures from outside. I invited Mr W. A. Lee and Mr A. J. Cook as the Secretaries respectively of the owners' and miners' associations; and two lawyer politicians, Sir Ellis Hume-Williams K.C., a Conservative M.P., and Mr E. G. Hemmerde K.C., one of the few barristers to

[1] Martin Gilbert, *Winston S. Churchill*, Heinemann, (1976), Vol. 5, p. 131.

[2] John Campbell, *F. E. Smith*, Jonathan Cape (1983) p. 777. See also John Bowle, *Viscount Samuel*, Gollancz (1957) p. 244.

have embraced Socialism. The motion would be proposed by Geoffrey Crowther and opposed by J. S. B. (in later life Selwyn) Lloyd, both then Liberals but of different persuasions.

I went up to Cambridge a week or so before term began so as to settle Union affairs. The lock-out was continuing though the miners had begun to drift back on the owners' terms. In August the Government had made a determined effort to bring it to an end. Mr Baldwin had withdrawn to Aix-les-Bains leaving the effort to Mr Churchill. He, who had been outstandingly aggressive for so long as the constitution was in danger, was now yielding to his lifelong inclination to magnanimity in victory. In September the governing factor was still the determined opposition of the owners to a national minimum. Churchill was ready 'to secure by legislation the main objects of a national settlement' and he drafted a letter to that effect.[1]

The most forcible opponent of a policy of conciliation was Lord Birkenhead. At an early stage he had singled out for attack my prospective guest, A. J. Cook. 'The only way', he had written on 24 June, 'of ending the coal strike is to break the Moscow disciple, Cook, who is directing it. I have, therefore, without much sanction from my colleagues, devoted my public speeches to an attempt to discredit him'.[2]

Cook was certainly an extremist and at the least a fellow-traveller. But there is nothing in the record of the negotiations to show that, as his enemies alleged, he was more concerned with the destruction of the coal industry than with securing a decent wage for his followers. He should be judged by that record rather then by the public oratory of a man who was now becoming desperate. But in the Cabinet, which lacked a clear lead from Mr Baldwin, the Birkenhead view prevailed at least to the point of a decision that owners and miners should be left to fight it out between themselves. This ensured the defeat of the miners. In the first week of October another 100,000 men went back to work. This was what Birkenhead wanted. 'The absolute defeat of the strike', he had written at the end of July, 'was necessary to educate the working people of this country into the iron reality of the economic wage'.[3]

The preaching of the Birkenhead gospel (and the bedevilling of Mr Cook) had, I found, caused considerable alarm among the burghers of Cambridge, remote though the borough was from any seedbed of revolution. I had a nodding acquaintance with a town councillor, a lawyer whom I had met at a university gathering. He called on me to explain the mayor's fears that a visit by Mr Cook

[1] Martin Gilbert, *Winston S. Churchill*, Heinemann, (1976), Vol.5, p. 205.

[2] John Campbell, *F. E. Smith*, Jonathan Cape, (1983), p. 777.

[3] John Campbell, ibid, p. 781.

would lead to rioting, broken windows and maybe much worse. 'So I said to him', he went on, 'Mr Mayor, let me handle this. Don't do anything drastic. I know Delvin very well,' I said. 'Delvin is a reasonable man and will see the point'. But Delvin did not see the point at all. There were not any miners in Cambridge to start the rioting. If there were any undergraduate thugs who wanted to start what they would call a bit of fun, this was a misfortune which a university town had to put up with.

Then I received a card from the Senior Proctor requesting or requiring me to call on him in his rooms at Emmanuel College. Since there was talk of rioting I thought it natural that he might wish to know what the Union was doing about it. I had had no dealings with the proctors before and did not allow my hypothesis to be displaced by the peremptory tone of the card or the inconvenience of the early hour named. The bleakness of the situation was revealed when I found myself detained in an ante-room and told to wait.

I was kept waiting for twenty minutes, fifteen of them after the appointed hour. Beyond the closed door, the proctor was sitting in solitude, for when eventually I was admitted there was no one but he in the room and no other door to it. It was not unusual in that decade for superiors whose manners were no better than their understanding to seek to impress their inferiors by keeping them waiting. In this case it was worse than a discourtesy; it was a blunder. It cost him the advantage of surprise. It gave me twenty minutes to consider how I could best behave in a surprise confrontation.

The proctor was sitting at a desk in front of which I was evidently expected to stand. I should like to be able to record that I at once demanded to know what delinquencies I was supposed to have committed; and that upon failing to receive a satisfactory answer, I turned on my heel and left the bully flabbergasted. It is today a commonplace that a person is entitled to know the charge against him before he is called upon to answer it. I dare say that even in 1926 an adult who was confident about his rights and ready to insist upon them would at a cost have ultimately prevailed. But in university life in 1926 there was a psychological barrier between those in *statu pupillari* and those in control. Proctorial powers were unquestioned. They could wreck a career. If I were to be sent down, three years at Cambridge would go for nothing: what would Uncle George say and what my father? What would Sir Geoffrey Butler say, he who had done so much? I feared – quite wrongly perhaps – that, if it came to taking sides, they would all be on the side of authority.

I had employed my twenty minutes in reaching three conclusions. First, to make it plain that the proctor was dealing not with an individual but with the agent of an institution that had been part of university life for over a century. Second, to offer nothing that could be represented as disrespect: that would be to provide him with the ammunition which, at present, he lacked. I must do nothing which could give him an incidental ground for complaint. The third was to say as little as possible. Silence that stops short of 'mute of malice'[1] is in these situations always the golden rule.

The proctor began by asking whether it was true that I had invited A. J. Cook to speak at the Union on 19th October: yes, it was. Cook, he went on, was a well-known agitator and he could not understand how I had been so foolish as to invite him. It was bound to lead to disorder and the consequences of that might be serious for me: I must now withdraw the invitation. He paused for a reply.

I answered that I would report what he had said to the Committee.

Was it not you yourself, he asked, who issued the invitation? I said that it was, but that the cancellation of an invitation which had been accepted was a different matter. There were three senior members of the Committee (the Treasurer, the Steward and the Librarian were all dons; normally they collogued separately with Mr Brown and rarely came to the Committee meetings) whom it would be at the very least discourteous not to consult.

The proctor shifted his ground to an implied acceptance of the possibility that the invitation might not be withdrawn. He said that I must understand that, if he had reason to fear disorder within the Union, he would enter the premises and restore order. I said that I did not anticipate disorder anywhere, but that I would report what he had said to the Committee. The meeting ended, as it had begun, without an exchange of customary politenesses.

I made my way to the Union and asked Mr Brown to summon an emergency meeting of the Committee. He regarded the proctorial intervention as one of those little troubles (Mr Macmillan as Prime Minister had yet to coin the phrase 'little local difficulties'[2]) that every president, he said, had to put up with. Some of them were recurrent, such as *The Pink 'Un*[3] – he would like to have a word with me about that. As to the Senior Proctor, he could not recollect the proctors giving any trouble before.

But when I told him that the proctor proposed to enter on the premises to restore order, he was shocked into animation. 'Leave him to me, sir', he said, 'I shall follow my usual practice. I shall ask him if he is a member; if he is not, I shall ask him to leave. If he brings his bulldogs[4] with him, of course they will have to go

---

[1] The common law is that, if on arraignment the prisoner stands mute, a jury must be empanelled to determine whether he is mute of malice or mute by the visitation of God.

[2] *Oxford Dictionary of Quotations*, 3rd edn., (1979), p. 325.

[3] This was a newspaper which filled its pages with racing news spiced, according to Mr Brown, with copious vulgarities. There was an annual demand, made usually in the Suggestion Book, that it should be one of the papers taken in by the Library. So far as I know, this was always successfully thwarted by Mr Brown.

[4] These were college servants of girth and speed who accompanied the proctors on their disciplinary expeditions.

at once. You keep out of it, sir. He cannot send *me* down. I shall tell him that there has never been any disorder in the Union in the twenty years that I have been here. I shall ask him, sir, if he can say the same of the Senate House.'[1]

At the meeting of the Committee no one suggested giving in to the proctor. No one anticipated any trouble from members of the Union, but it was thought that admission to the premises should be screened. Some of the Committee had heard talk of a rag, kidnapping Mr Cook at the railway station or something like that. Mr Brown thought that it would be quite simple to have him brought to the Union by car; there had been an occasion when an unpopular politician had been admitted unobtrusively. I emphasized the need for silence; we must not let anything get about that might discourage Mr Cook from coming.

Alas. A few days later Mr Cook wrote to say that it had become impossible for him to fulfil his engagement. I have no doubt at all that it was genuinely impossible for him to take time off from rallying his dispirited troops. Another 100,000 had gone back in October. Indeed there were only a few more weeks to go before his capitulation. Walter Citrine[2], Secretary of the T.U.C. Council, was good enough to accept an invitation to take Mr Cook's place. His magnificent speech was probably responsible for the size of the minority vote. The motion for the diminishment of trade unionism was carried by 378 votes to 237.

This episode was a valuable experience. It has enabled me to understand the sort of helplessness in the face of authority which the lawyer, familiar with the legal rights of the citizen, may dismiss too easily. It was also my first example of that difficult concept, conduct likely to lead to a breach of the peace, and of its potentiality as a suppressive of free speech. I disapprove wholeheartedly of the behaviour of some university students who are led to break the peace by the expression of views with which they disagree. But I do not forget that my first encounter with intimidation involved not the immature student but the Senior Proctor of the University of Cambridge.

The President of the Union is given the opportunity of meeting informally the established figures in the world in which he hopes to move. Breakfast was then, at the university, a social meal; a visitor to the Union who had not got to take the early train back to London was happy to accept an invitation to breakfast with the President in his rooms. On this first occasion Sir Ellis Hume-Williams came and, having disposed of the bacon and eggs, talked a lot about himself, a subject in which I was almost as interested as he was, for he was the lawyer-politician coming to the end of a career. He had made a very successful speech in the debate, displaying all

---

[1] This was a shrewd reminder of the disturbances in the Senate House over the proposal that women should be admitted to University degrees.

[2] Later Lord Citrine 1887-1983.

the graces which the Union likes to see; the speech was, as the second Lord Russell of Killowen once put it, as enjoyable as the flame around the Christmas pudding, adorning the subject without consuming it.

I remember Sir Ellis as an elegant figure with an easy and wave-of-the-hand manner. His life had been in the law and in politics. He fought his first election, standing as a Conservative of course, as soon as he had established himself as a junior at the Bar, but he did not get into the House until 1910 when he had been in silk for eleven years. He never wanted to be a judge, but he would have liked to have been a law officer. His chance did not come until 1922, when Bonar Law came in after the fall of the Lloyd George coalition. He was then 59. His friends told him that his claim was irresistible, but younger men were preferred.[1] He was consoled with a baronetcy and had no hard feelings about it. But this would be his last parliament. (He did in fact retire after the 1929 election, was made a privy councillor, wrote his memoirs and lived on, I expect contentedly, until 1947.)

I made four out of the eight debates political and four non-political. The first of the non-political was on a delicate subject but one which I thought ought to be discussed at a university. 'That the presence of oriental students at English universities cannot promote a better understanding between East and West'. Half a century has driven the colour bar, the most insensate of British prejudices, out of the light and into the shadows. But in 1926 it was as rigid in Cambridge, notwithstanding that it was a university, as everywhere else. Though there were many Indian students at Cambridge, they had their own club, the Majlis, and they mixed hardly at all with the general body. The question was whether the university was – in reality and not just ideally – the best place in which to dig at the roots of prejudice. H. M. Foot[2] proposed the motion in a skilful speech. 'Eastern and Western cultures were essentially different' he said 'and nowhere were they less likely to be reconciled than in the atmosphere of youthful intolerance prevalent at a university'. But the voting, 239 to 42, went very decisively against him. There was an Indian speaker on each side. R. A. Gopalaswami, perhaps the most eloquent speaker of his time who has since played a distinguished part in Indian administrative life, was the opposer; at the end of the term he was elected to the Committee.

The fourth debate was on a motion deploring 'the prominence given to questions of sex in the post-war novel'. I suppose that the defeat of the motion by 296 votes to 210 may be taken as showing how far the permissive society had crept

[1] So it was his successful rivals who made off with the spoils. They both became Lord Chancellors and viscounts (Hailsham and Caldecote) and one of them Lord Chief Justice to boot.

[2] Later Lord Caradon.

in by 1926. I had invited J. C. Squire[1] to support the motion and Compton Mackenzie[2] to oppose it. Both made fine speeches. They came to breakfast the next morning. Squire asked for mutton chops and a pint of ale which the college kitchen readily provided. Their conversation was delightful and their offer to propose and second me for the Savile Club very tempting.

The fifth debate took place after the 5th November. That date, as is well known, is often commemorated by the sort of collective misbehaviour which even without the stimulus of a Mr Cook can attract the undergraduate mind. This was what was to be discussed on the motion that 'the amusements of the undergraduate are too frequently injudicious'. The audience showed a lack of collective repentance by rejecting the motion by 142 votes to 107. This in spite of a powerful speech by Michael Ramsey when he recounted an incident in which 'he was addressing a political meeting from a cart and a member of the proletariat told the horse to "gee up"'. *Query:* could this have had any significance on his subsequent choice of the pulpit as a firmer base for his mature oratory?)

The last of the non-political debates was on the sort of subject which it is the duty of the universities to provide from time to time for the benefit of the national press: that 'this House disapproves of Woman'. 'BANGLED, BINGLED AND BUNGLED' the dailies shrieked: the Secretary, M. A .B. King-Hamilton, had given them just what was needed: 'she bangles her arms' he declared, 'bingles her hair and bungles her face'. This was the gleeful side. There was also heavy gunfire from the correspondence columns; do these young men appreciate that, were it not for women, they would not be there to debate? Sociologists may care to know that the motion was defeated by 191 votes to 164.

In November there were two events which I remember vividly. On the 23rd we had a political debate to which the Marquess of Londonderry came to speak for the Conservative side. The Master of Christ's had said to me at the beginning of the term that he would be pleased to have for the night any guest whom I was inviting to speak at the Union, adding as a clarification (which I did not need) 'anyone important of course I mean'. Sir Arthur Shipley, a distinguished zoologist, was a small fat man with a moustache that was rather too big for him. When he was Vice-Chancellor he had his portrait painted in robes by Laszlo[3] with a dozen or so smaller reproductions of it nicely framed. He gave me one of these. I liked him and he quite liked me. In his dealings with undergraduates he was selective with a tendency towards the Lapsley principle; there were not many of the well-born at Christ's and he had to make do with the other two categories. He gave large parties

---

[1] Sir John Squire, writer, (1884-1958).

[2] Sir Compton Mackenzie, author, (1883-1972).

[3] Philip de Laszlo, FRSA, Painter (1869-1937).

occasionally. The Master's Lodge is a fine house with fine rooms; in the twenties it was even finer, for it then included the large room that after his time became the Senior Combination Room. But he entertained mostly with luncheons for six or eight in the small dining room which is now the Master's study. I met my first Cabinet Minister there and on another occasion my first Lord Chancellor.

I reckoned that Lord Londonderry would rank as someone important, which he did. The Master did not care for having even important people to breakfast. But this guest had only to step across the threshold of the Lodge to reach my rooms and he breakfasted with me. He was one of the largest of the coal owners and so under Lord Birkenhead's dictum the possessor of a stupidity exceeding that of the miners'. Whether or not that was so in industrial matters, he was a most pleasant and forthcoming guest.

He sent me a card for the reception at Londonderry House in Park Lane which he gave every year for the Opening of Parliament. It was an event belonging to the world which ended in 1939. The backbone of a great reception, the broad flight of stairs and the ballroom or the picture gallery, are no longer part of even the largest private house. The diamond tiaras must still be about but languishing; there are not enough occasions to bring them out into the open; disuse tempts their owners to turn them into something more practical. Court dress for the gentleman was in 1926 no longer *de rigueur* but dress uniforms were not only naval or military: privy councillors wore them and the royal household; so did ambassadors and the like. Anyway, what was essential to the good appearance of the male was the right length of the coat which at some point must descend to the knees. The swallowtail coat of the period was perfectly elegant, giving length without weightiness, but it had to be perfectly cut. The jacket simply would not do. Nor would the soft shirt. The starched shirt, collar and cuffs, ridiculous in themselves, were basic to the ensemble and to the display of orders and decorations. I am glad not to have missed a sight of a combination of splendours that can now be seen only as reconstructed for television.

By recalling myself to the memory of the notables whom I had met in Cambridge I found that I knew enough people to give me a very enjoyable evening. I got some advice from Mr Churchill which I have not taken. 'You should go into politics' he said. 'Fight an East End constituency and learn to use your fists as well as your tongue.'

I was invited to luncheon at Londonderry House the next day. It seems incredible that it was within the reach of a private establishment, after encompassing a reception for several hundred guests on the previous evening, to serve a luncheon for a couple of dozen on the next day. I do not now recollect anything about it except the charm of Lady Londonderry who was supposed at this time to be holding captive in her silken web the Socialist leader, Ramsay Macdonald. If this is true, I can only say that there was also room in her web for the least important of her guests.

The other event was in a minor key. Thursday 25 November, falling between the sixth and seventh debates, was my twenty-first birthday. It is not often that this occurs during a presidency and it made an occasion, Mr Brown thought, for displaying the resources of the Union; the committee room he said, could be made available. I chose the dinner under the wise guidance of the steward, A. T. Bartholomew of Peterhouse, the first in my life of many enjoyable discussions of what to eat and drink. He recommended a champagne of 1911, *Duc de Montebello*, which he said had been favoured by King Edward VII. There were fourteen places, so the company had to be restricted to the best of my friends. I asked Uncle Theodore to preside. He approved of the company and enjoyed the reincarnation of his Oxford days. His hosting was not merely nominal, for his birthday cheque of £15 just about paid for the dinner.

The freshmen of 1923 made a good year for the Union. An average annual intake ought to produce three presidents: 1923 produced five, filling its quota for 1926-27 and spilling over into the year before and the year after. Two of the five were of exceptional distinction and they were the overspills, Michael Ramsey the Archbishop of Canterbury and 'Peter' (as we called him then), later Selwyn Lloyd who became in succession Foreign Secretary, Chancellor of the Exchequer and Speaker of the House of Commons, while Rab Butler, the nearest the Cambridge Union has come to begetting a Prime Minister, was just outside the intake. I have not said much about Peter. I did not know him very well until my last year when we went together up to London quite frequently to eat our dinners at Gray's Inn. He was a slow starter, painfully shy and he did not sparkle; grit and perseverance and loyalty took him to the heights. As I wrote to him when he achieved the last of his offices, any one of us in his young and ambitious days would have settled gladly with the god of fortune for any one of the three places and he had them all.

Then there were those who would become President and who were in full vigour in my last year. The three of them whom I knew best at Cambridge and afterwards were Hugh Foot, later Lord Caradon, and Geoffrey (later Lord) Crowther who edited the *Economist* from 1938 to 1956. These two became men of national renown. Robert Stevenson was one of the non-political presidents. He went into films and was an immediate success as a director, making his first film in 1932. He had a house, I remember, by the side of the Thames on the south bank. Then he went to Hollywood where he had a great success and is now remembered chiefly for *Mary Poppins*. He set out to please and he did in his life as well as in his films.

There were also those who took the Union less seriously but who liked to speak from time to time. Three contemporaries went, like myself, into the law and on to the judicial bench. Roger Winn, a double first in classics and law, became a Lord Justice of Appeal. Bernard Gillis and Alan King-Hamilton became Old Bailey judges sitting there contemporaneously for fifteen years. Bob (P. J. or Pierson) Dixon,[1] a particular friend, was the earliest among us to play a part in great affairs. He was a brilliant classical scholar who went into the diplomatic service. As private secretary to Sir Anthony Eden he was active at Yalta in 1945 and ended his career as our ambassador at Paris. Hugh Caradon and he were at different times ambassadors to the United Nations.

Then there was Gilbert Harding who in his short public life (he died when he was fifty-three) established himself as one of the high eccentrics of the age. He first came to my notice at the Union when at a private business meeting he moved for the appointment of a select committee 'to consider the advisability of a robe of suitably dignified colour and design to be worn by the President'. He was a frequent debater. When he went down he worked his way up from schoolmaster to police constable to *Times* correspondent. In one of the early debates in my term I wrote of him in the *Cambridge Review* that he should not submit so mildly to his interrupters: that must have been the making of him. Within a shell of false surliness there was much to admire and to like.

I had not been neglecting my tripos but until I finished the course of office at the Union I had always in my mind the procrastinating thought that after Christmas I would have six months to devote entirely to the law. But how does one set about preparing for an examination? I have no idea now and I had none then. What I lacked was an object. At the Bar when I knew that I had on the next day or in the following week to make an opening speech or cross-examine a witness, I never had any difficulty in absorbing the necessary material, whether it was fact or law. Likewise on the Bench if I had to deliver an unreserved judgment or a summing up. What makes that sort of work easy and interesting is that every bit of material as it comes in is either given an immediate place in the structure or else asked to take a seat in the waiting room as there may be a short delay until a vacancy is found. If it is not wanted, it goes into a limbo where its existence may or may not be forgotten.

I have found this a satisfactory way of working in professional life. But it is no sort of preparation for an examination paper in which you are asked to supply within the next three hours information on a variety of topics of which you have been given no previous notice. That is a demand which is never made in real life except to an expert in a narrow field. It is no fit conclusion to a university education. If it were not for this fantastic way of ending it, university life would be

[1] Consult the indexes in Martin Gilbert, *Winston S. Churchill*, Heinemann, 1986 and Robert Rhodes James, *Anthony Eden*, George Weidenfeld & Nicolson.

as agreeable as it is profitable. Learning comes by reading books and discussing them. As it seeps in, the level slowly rises in the well to the point at which one can happily dip and drink. But the well is not like the hump on the camel's back. It is not portable and cannot be piped to the human head. For happy drinking the pupil must go to it.

This was the sort of happiness that Arthur Goodhart knew how to provide. Then there was Harry Hollond at Trinity who, although his hands were full, agreed to take me for Real Property. Jack Hamson was at this time still in the course of acquiring his double first in classics. But already he had begun to relish a discussion about life terms and remainders, vested and contingent, and enjoyed hearing about the way in which Harry Hollond would immediately after a hypothetical death set about carving up the estate. This was the early sign of his conversion to the law which led speedily to a fellowship at Trinity and eventually to the chair of Comparative Law.

Supervision over all was lacking. The nearest I got to it was with a Mr Herdman. He had an old friendship with D. T. Oliver[1], a tutor at Trinity Hall and a lecturer on Personal Property. His old friend put him in the way of some teaching work; he had gone to the Bar in Northern Ireland, but I suspect that like my father he lacked the aptitude for getting on in life. He was an excellent teacher and he had a nimble mind which in tutoring Arthur Goodhart had not. This was surprising for nimbleness usually goes with the quick wit which Arthur displayed in conversation and in after dinner speeches. But not in discussion of legal principles. Nor in matters concerning the Pedestrians' Association of which he was president for twelve years, during which it was not safe to mention any speed over 35 mph. One learnt from him by absorption and not by argument. Herdman was always ready for an argument, though Alan King-Hamilton (he and I went for supervision together) recalls that I was frequently rebuked for 'chasing hares'.

So the first part of 1927 was devoted to law; I stayed in Cambridge for most of the Easter vacation so as to be able to work with the books. Not long before the examination began I got a hunch. One three hour paper was allotted to an essay. Arthur said that it was not intended to test literary powers; no trills or tropes would be expected. There would be a choice of four or five subjects, the object being to inspect the examinee's field of knowledge rather more extensively than could be done through the ordinary question. My hunch was that one of the subjects would be Contracts in Restraint of Trade.

As the days passed my hunch was elevated to the closest I have ever experienced to a revelation. Indeed the thing became a certainty. I memorised all the leading cases with their names and dates. I hesitated to contemplate what would befall me

---

[1] The father of Lord Oliver of Aylmerton, a Lord of Appeal.

if my faith was betrayed. It was not. Contracts in Restraint of Trade was there. I hardly noticed what the other subjects were. I wrote and wrote.

Uncle George planned to spend a few days in Cambridge. The time that suited him was about the time when the tripos results came out, so I decided to await him there. His main object in coming south was to spend a couple of weeks at Droitwich, a town in Worcestershire with brine baths and a reputation as a health resort. There was a doctor there who would give him treatment for his leg. It sounded as bad as the rack, pulling and stretching the limb.

This added a particular horror to a venture which he was perhaps already regretting. He had just bought a small Rolls-Royce, the 20 hp model. It had of course every comfort obtainable in that age, as indeed it should have in exchange for the substantial price of £2,000, including, if I remember rightly, a device for re-starting the engine if it stalled in traffic: no need any more to jump out with the starting handle. So he had been tempted to take the Rolls and go by road.

But he was now over fifty and had reached prematurely the age when a holiday becomes only a deprivation of routine. He had decided to take Duncan with him as he might well not want to drive himself all the way, especially after Droitwich. This decision was not soundly based. I doubt that he had ever been driven by Duncan for any distance. At home he always drove himself everywhere; when he bought his first car, he had driven it out of the shop. He very rarely exceeded 20 or 30 miles a day. Duncan's function was to bring the car to the door in the morning and to put it away in the evening; and of course to look after it which he did perfectly.

Duncan was a man who would have been highly esteemed by Arthur Goodhart's Pedestrians' Association. He had taught me to drive and I knew that he thought it wrong – indeed, wicked – to exceed 20 mph. This was the legal speed limit until 1934. Britain would not be Britain if there were not at least one law on the statute book which only an eccentric observed. No others took 20 mph seriously, not even the police.

I knew that Duncan held his opinion tenaciously, though whether out of respect for the law or because of a feeling that she (Duncan always referred to the car as 'she') should be treated with every consideration, rather as Aunt Connie treated Jeannie, I did not know. I had mentioned the idiosyncracy to Uncle George but he simply refused to credit it. He had a justifiably low opinion of my mechanical abilities and I am not sure that he was totally convinced that I could read a speedometer correctly.

In any circumstances Uncle George disliked being driven instead of driving; to be driven at 20 mph infuriated him. Duncan was respectful but unyielding, as obdurate as only a Scot can be on a matter of minor principle. So Uncle George

71

drove from Droitwich to Cambridge himself with a leg that was, I am sure, very painful. When he arrived in Cambridge, he was exhausted, still in constant pain and without his usual rituals to observe horribly bored. The only things we had to talk about were the expected tripos results and whether I had any debts.

On the first topic I felt that it was not a moment for a display, genuine or unfeigned, of pessimism. My prospects of a first had been thought to be good and with the almost unbelievable piece of luck over the essay I felt that it could be taken as safe. I did not suppose that it greatly mattered to my career whether I got a first, a second or a third and in fact I cannot think of anyone who has had the curiosity to inquire. But it was evident that I needed another feather in my cap and to dispel the gloom I spoke expansively.

Tripos results were put up outside the Senate House at 8.00 am. I got up early to get the news and take it to breakfast with Uncle George at the University Arms. Mine was not among the three or four names in the first division of the first class. I had not expected that. But I was bitterly disappointed when it was not to be found in the second division (of the first class) and could hardly believe my eyes when it was not among the crowd in the first division of the second class. After that it did not matter much whether it was a second or a third. In fact it was a 'two-two'.

At the breakfast table Uncle George neither commiserated nor reproached. It was not his habit to do either. But as one apparently concerned only with the practical consequences he wanted to know what now were my plans and he inquired in a manner that made it quite plain that, as was only too true, he had committed himself to nothing.

There was his other question for which I ought to have been prepared but was not: what were my debts? I ought to have anticipated that because it was a subject that was something of an obsession with the parental generation of my time. It was axiomatic that to be in debt was a dreadful thing. The entry of the bailiffs and the foreclosing of the mortgage were dooms explored extensively in pre-1914 fiction as was the slippery path to the moneylender which the young were regularly implored never to take. True that in 1927 Maynard Keynes was in residence at King's, already famous for his *Economic Consequences of the Peace* but not yet for his ideas about borrowing the way to prosperity. Today we all know that behind the villainous mask of the money lender there is the beaming face of a bank manager with his pressing offer of a student's overdraft. But in 1927 there was nothing like that, no more than a recognition that boys would be boys (nothing, of course, about girls being girls) so that an indulgent view could be taken of some moderate grasshopping before a full acceptance of the destiny of the ant. But an essential preliminary to the indulgence was the sort of disclosure that the tax inspector demands before the remission of penalties.

A younger brother whose victimisation by primogeniture was, save in the landed gentry, never very severe, always has the advantage of the experience paid for by the eldest. When seven years later my brother Bill came down from Oxford I warned him of what was expected and he was able to produce a list and then a supplementary list and received a cheque for the full amount. I was taken by surprise. I had certainly not resisted the temptations of credit so easily obtained from Cambridge tailors. While in other respects I had not balanced my books, I had no doubt that there would be a deficit. I was also conscious that I had been treated generously by Uncle George in my last year. In recognition of the fact that I was President of the Union my allowance had been increased to £350. So I was left to pay my own debts.

As to the future, my plan was to spend a year in a solicitor's office in London; I shall explain in the next chapter how that came to be formed. Did I expect to earn anything that year? Uncle George inquired. The answer was only what I might pick up if I was lucky enough to get a few odd jobs. And when did I expect to keep myself? There were then very few penniless barristers, only those with solicitor's patronage secured by blood relationship, who could give a satisfactory answer to that; the best that could be manufactured out of bleak uncertainties would have to do.

It would be two years before I was called. After that the advice I had got was that it would be at best three years and at worst seven before I was earning a livelihood. 'At worst' does not mean that after seven years a livelihood was guaranteed, but that, if I was not by then making a good enough income, I had better throw in my hand and look for one of the comfortable jobs open to those who were not failures. Of course one could hold on: 'Look at Jones who must now be making £30,000 a year if he's making a penny and who earned less than a hundred guineas in his first ten years.'

I do not think that I managed either of these subjects, the career or the debts, with skill. No decision was conveyed. But it looked as if a year in London, if granted, would be, as it were, probationary. And Uncle George expressed a firm view that £200 would be a sufficient allowance. He added that if I made any earnings, I could keep them.

During the next few days I meditated profoundly on this situation. Between me and the service of the law there was no pledge. When a man has a vocation he has to answer the call and the call commands his life: if he ignores it he will not be happy. I had no vocation and so had a field of choice. It was not constricted by any personal or family obligation. What factors should govern the choice? I reached then a conclusion from which I have not varied that the aim should be to obtain the greatest enjoyment out of life.

To say this at once makes people think of a life of idleness or of so-called pleasure without work. This is nonsense. There is no pleasure except in a life of occupation. The essential pleasure in life is to be obtained only from congenial work. That must be the sun that heats the spirit. But there are planetary pleasures which make a very significant contribution to enjoyment and most of them need money.

Moreover, since man lives in the spirit as well as in the flesh, life would not be congenial unless it could be seen as in some sort a pursuit of virtue. The virtue which most like to pursue is charity, which can be modernised as social service. The emotion which powers it is compassion. For me the virtue is justice which is powered by a colder emotion, the root of which is a love of the order that moves the universe and which is an aspect of godliness. Compassion and justice are very compatible but, if forced to choose, I would rather be just than compassionate.

But just men do not need to be lawyers nor do they need to sacrifice the planetary pleasures. The Bar would not mean a total sacrifice but it would mean a long postponement, a sentence not of death but of up to ten years' servitude from which I should emerge in my thirties. To require the loss of what made youth enjoyable was to ask too much. I supposed that one could live in London on £200 a year but it would be a mean life; and moreover an uncertain life without tenure, renewable from year to year. I did not think it was a life for me. There must be other chances and a less lugubrious way of getting on in the world. I did not believe that my rank in life was in the second division of the second class.

I never found out for certain how I came to be there. I am told that today an open policy is favoured and that examinees are given their marks on each paper. But in 1927 the strictest secrecy was observed. Hints and ambiguities were the best that could be hoped for and they were obtainable only from someone highly accredited. Arthur Goodhart made a few casts into these murky waters. What he told me much later confounded me. It was hinted that what had let me down was the essay. When I told Arthur the circumstances that made this quite impossible, he wondered, having had some experience of my handwriting, whether excitement might not have rushed it headlong into illegibility.

I have never had a hunch before or since and I hope that I shall never have another.

Chapter VI

LONDON

TO BE CALLED to the Bar at this time it was necessary to join an Inn of Court, pass some examinations, – not at all difficult – and keep twelve terms, four to a year, which was done by eating dinners in the Hall, three to each term. It was also considered necessary, though not compulsory, to do a year's pupillage in the chambers of a practising barrister. So I had a year to spare before I could be called and I was advised that it could be usefully spent in a solicitors' office in London.

This would be substantially more expensive than living at Cambridge. There were of course university and college fees to pay in Cambridge while there were few fees that had to be paid in London. A Cambridge degree exempted the holder from most of the Bar examinations and the rest could be got quite easily from books. Or so I thought: in fact I failed in constitutional law on my first attempt and had to take the subject again. So I went to a coach who himself had got a first in all his Bar examinations. To follow his teachings did not require a first-class mind. From a close and careful study of examination papers he said that he would be able to tell with a 50% chance of success what the questions in each subject would be. I studied the model answers to each of these questions and in this way secured a third-class in the examination.

I had fixed on £400 a year as the amount which would secure me in the state of life to which I had become accustomed. I took the problem to Sir Geoffrey Butler and he advised me to talk to Arthur Goodhart. He was not deterred by poor results in my finals and said that I must go to the Bar. He said that he could find things for me to do for the *Law Quarterly Review* which he edited and would pay me £200 a year for the two years until I was called. This was marvellous. I never lost touch with Sir Geoffrey who thought of all the small things as well as big. On his advice the following Christmas I sent a box of chocolates from Charbonnel and Walker to Mr Goodhart and Mr Withers.[1]

I think that Uncle George certainly, and to an extent Arthur Goodhart, supposed that a call to the Bar meant a self-supporting income beginning at once. I knew very well that it did not and that it would be prudent to put aside part of the money I was getting to help with the first years at the Bar. So, in this summer of 1927, I set about looking for somewhere to live in London. I saw an advertisement for

[1] Refer page 80.

unfurnished rooms in Half Moon Street. I ought to have averted my gaze and looked for furnished rooms in Bloomsbury, convenient for Gray's Inn and the Temple, but I did not. Half Moon Street, besides having a name redolent of London before the War, is one of the three small streets, – Clarges and Down being the others – which run north from Piccadilly opposite the Green Park into Curzon Street. They were in 1929 all small houses except for Flemings Hotel about half way up. In the basement there was a kitchen and some rooms for the couple who ran the house. The ground and first floors were two very pleasant, self-contained flats – perhaps the third was too. But after the third a narrow staircase led up to the unfurnished rooms in the advertisement which were small sitting-room, bedroom and bathroom. £4 per week was quite a reasonable rent to pay for them. As for the furniture I was told that in the antique shops in Praed Street and in Church Street in Kensington you could buy period and reproduction furniture at very reasonable prices. I have still a few of the things that I bought and their annual insurance premium now is about ten times their cost then.

So I discontinued my journey to Bloomsbury and settled for Mayfair instead.

While I was still at 21 Half Moon Street I met a neighbour at No. 20. This does not usually happen in Mayfair – at any rate until after a substantial period of mutual observation. No. 20 was occupied as a whole house by an Italian called Romolo Piazzani. He had an establishment somewhere in South Kensington where he sold very expensive furniture and he also advised on the decoration of interiors. I think that this was a hobby rather than a means of support for he was not very often at the shop. His main interest was in giving rather select parties. There are usually to be found in London a small number of minor royalties who have nothing to do and are quite pleased to go out to dinner at suitable houses recommended by their ladies-in-waiting. Mr Piazzani had arranged in this manner a dinner party for Princess Andrew of Greece. He liked to give a sort of *conversazione* flavour to his entertainments and had a young friend called Hamilton Kerr who had just come down from Oxford and wanted to start a political career who was to be one of the guests. He came one evening to No. 20 to discuss the project and took with him Peter Herbert, a friend of Piazzani's.

The idea emerged that there would be a debate on some current political topic which Hamilton Kerr would initiate. Early in the discussion the objection was raised that Princess Andrew was deaf. But this was overruled when Peter pointed out that this made entertainment all the more necessary since otherwise she would have to be continuously engaged in single-handed conversation. They then cast around the list of guests to find another suitable debater but were unsuccessful.

Then Peter remembered that I had given him an address in London which he thought was Half Moon Street. He found his book and, lo and behold, the address was next door. Mr Piazzani then demurred because he had filled his table and unless someone fell through I could not be invited to dinner. Peter said that I would not mind that since I lived next door and that they had all better go and find out. So all three of them came and in this way I made two new and very agreeable friends.

I have forgotten entirely about the debate and what, if anything, we discussed. But among the other guests I met Mrs Anthony Henley, a widow with three daughters, the eldest of whom, Rosalind, came with her. Her husband, who had been killed in the war had been in peace time the military secretary to Mr Asquith when he was Prime Minister. Mr Asquith, as is now well known, liked pretty young women and liked in particular Mrs Henley's younger sister, Venetia Stanley. Their correspondence fills a large volume and has proved of great interest to historians. She and her two elder daughters, Rosalind and Kitty, became very firm friends. She had a house in Bayswater, 9 Oxford Square, at which she entertained a great deal and through them I met many other people.

One of Rosalind's great friends was Miriam Rothschild. Concealed behind their very good-looking appearances was the fact that they were both devoting their lives to two scientific subjects which they never mentioned to me and which I do not suppose I would have understood if they had. But while spending most of the day being entertained or entertaining as if they had nothing else to do in the world, they were both actively engaged in their studies, Rosalind at Bedford College. Rosalind became F.R.S. and Miriam[1] is a great authority on fleas. The Rothschilds had one of those large houses in Kensington Palace Gardens; there was a house also at Tring where old Lady Rothschild lived and sometimes talked about Disraeli and another in Northamptonshire not too far for weekends.

What Talleyrand called *la douceur de vivre* ended in 1914. The decline was in two stages. In the first stage the slope was much gentler than in the second. Between 1919 and 1939 life for the rich was different, but not catastrophically different, from what it had been before the war. Income tax was between 4s and 5s in the pound and there was no VAT. More important than that prices had not enormously increased. The wages payable in domestic service for example were about double what they had been before 1914, but the double was still not very high. £80–£90 per year for a really good cook with board and lodging (say half a bedroom) was the usual. A stall in a theatre was 12s 6d (that is 60p) and so on. People still lived in large London houses and gave dinner parties for a dozen or more and even "small dances", a term which covered everything that was not a "ball". This was the background of my social life.

I have mentioned the occasion at Cambridge when after the debate on sex in the

[1] Miriam Rothschild was elected F.R.S. in 1985.

modern novel Compton MacKenzie and Jack Squire came to breakfast with me. They said that when I came to live in London I ought to join the Savile Club of which they were both members. It was a club in Piccadilly for "men of letters". The lease of the Piccadilly premises was running out and, in order to find a suitable house, they had to look to the north of Mayfair beyond the area where clubs were usually to be found. They had found a suitable house in Brook Street. The Guards Club was in Brook Street, but apart from that it was only on the fringe of what the press called "West End Clubland". 69 Brook Street was larger than their Piccadilly house so they wanted to increase their membership and were on the look-out for suitable candidates for whom they would probably remit the entrance fee. So when I had settled in Half Moon Street I wrote to Jack Squire (Compton Mackenzie was always floating about from one remote residence, probably in the north of Scotland, to another on a small island somewhere near Guernsey) and he arranged it all.

For a few months I was happy in Half Moon Street. The problem for a young man in those days in London was what to do in the evenings and for me that was spending too much money. In Bloomsbury, no doubt, I should have been surrounded by contemporaries leading the hard life. There were not it is true many contemporaries living in Mayfair except one or two in Shepherd Market which was considered to be a dubious area. But many belonged to the clubs and there were many small restaurants, especially in Soho, where one could easily meet with a friend for dinner. The couple in Half Moon Street were supposed to provide meals at a reasonable charge and I daresay that they did so for the more opulent inhabitants in the ground and first floor flats. But the man was not attracted by the idea of bringing any very elaborate meal up four flights of stairs and the woman was not at all a good cook. She looked to me as if she might have escaped from Shepherd Market and at any rate in the genteel phrase common in those days was 'no better than she should be!' Life in 21 Half Moon Street was not what I had expected.

I quite often dined at the Savile. There was a table d'hôte dinner for 4s 6d and a long table where members usually sat if they had not brought a guest. No. 69 Brook Street consisted of two large houses which had been thrown into one to accommodate Lord and Lady Harcourt. Harcourt was the son of the Victorian statesman who had been in Gladstone's Cabinets at the end of the century and who had, when the old man went, been defeated for the leadership of the Liberal Party by Rosebery. The Harcourts were descended from an old family which had produced many distinguished figures, including a Lord Chancellor, but who had not, by the end of the nineteenth century, very much money left. Lulu Harcourt, the eldest son of Sir William, had, as was the prudent custom in those days, married a rich American. No. 69 was arranged to suit her requirements. The ground floor and the first floor of one house were altered to provide a large and imposing staircase with two wings which met at the ballroom on the first floor.

Altogether there were many more bedrooms than the Club needed or than it wanted to furnish at a time when its resources had already been strained to acquire the Harcourt residence. When I approached the Secretary to enquire about the possibility of having a room in the Club for longer than the usual week or fortnight, he was delighted to hear that I was in a position to furnish it. He took me up to the second floor where Lady Harcourt had had her suite. There was a large room which had been turned into the Club Library. It looked out on the back secluded from the noise, – such as it then was, – of Brook Street traffic, – it had been Lady Harcourt's bedroom. Opposite and looking out over Brook Street there was what had been her dressing room or boudoir. She had had one corner of it made into a bathroom and the whole redecorated in the Empire style fashionable in those days, green and gold moulding.

The historian interested in reconstructing the scenario which I am now describing can, no doubt, easily get access to the public rooms of the Savile Club - the double staircase and the ballroom – but perhaps not so easily to the bedrooms. But if he turns south out of Brook Street into Davies Street and crosses diagonally Berkeley Square and if, but only if, he has booked a table in the Connaught Grill he will see the green and gold decor exactly as it was, and maybe still is, in Lady Harcourt's boudoir. The furniture I had was not unsuited to the decor. A lacquer bureau and a joss-table fitted in quite nicely.

I have forgotten just what I paid but it was somewhere between £2 and £3 a week and this was including all the amenities of Club service. I lived there for four years until the time of my marriage. Then my wife-to-be, though females were strictly forbidden in the club, was allowed in by devious ways to inspect the furniture I had and pronounce it suitable for the house we were buying in Westminster, 65 Romney Street.

My friends in London to begin with were mostly those whom I had met at Cambridge in my last year. Rab and Sydney Butler continued to live in London when they were not in the country in Rab's constituency. They bought there a small house in the country called Broxted Hall and made it very attractive turning an old brewhouse into a large room. The railway station was Elsenham between Bishop's Stortford and Audley End so it was easy to get to and from London where they spent most weekends.

For some time I had an arrangement with Alick Dru, a friend belonging to the Downside group at Cambridge, by which we dined once a week at each other's clubs. He belonged to the St James' Club where the cuisine was superior to that of the Savile. After a bit we settled down to a dinner on Sunday evening at the St James'. We each paid half the bill.

Evelyn Waugh was a member of the Savile Club and, like myself, lived there for a short time after his first marriage had split in 1929. He had already published *Decline and Fall* and *Vile Bodies* followed in 1930. When the club emptied after dinner we used to sit on and talk. His talk was a point or two lower than his writing which I greatly admire.

I remember one evening when he took me to a party somewhere in Maida Vale. I think his object in taking me was so that I would pay at least half of the taxi fare. There were only a very few people there in a small room with a table in the middle on which there was a bowl. In the bowl there were newspaper clippings. The guests dipped their fingers and pulled out one of the clippings which I took to be reviews of a book which our host had written.

This could, I suppose, have made a subject for conversation but there was an attractive girl lying on the floor; there was no surplus of chairs. I spent a very agreeable time talking to her and then we left. She was, I think, one of the Lygon sisters. Evelyn told me in the taxi that she was "somebody or other's" girl which I assumed to be a warning off the course.

I must turn now to the more serious side of my London life.

In January 1926 Mr Rawlinson MP died. He was one of the two university representatives in Parliament. His death was followed by a search for a successor. John Withers was a successful London solicitor in his fifties. He had been at King's to which he was devoted and this quite often brought him to Cambridge. He had helped St Catherine's with their affairs and they had made him an honorary fellow. The caucus invited him to fill the vacancy.

When I was discussing with Sir Geoffrey the idea of going to the Bar and I had explained to him that I would have a year to fill in (the other year would be my pupillage) and told him that people advised that a good way of filling it in would be at a solicitor's office – he thought that Withers was just the man. Withers, he had been told, was the sort of solicitor who could make a young man going to the Bar. Approached in this way, Withers agreed to take me and to waive the hundred guineas which was the normal fee for the year's pupillage.

Accordingly on some morning towards the end of September 1927 I presented myself at the office of Withers. It was in an old fashioned house at the bottom or lower end of Arundel Street which descended from the Strand to the Embankment at the Temple station on the Underground.

Withers was one of the three big firms of what were called West End solicitors, dealing with society business rather than commercial. The other two were Charles Russell and Company, which had a good deal of privy council work from Canada especially and had been started by a Russell related to the Chief Justice at the beginning of the century. The other was Lewis and Lewis, well known for the activities of the first Sir George Lewis who played a considerable part in rescuing indiscreet letters from Edward VII to his mistresses when he was Prince of Wales. Withers had started the firm with his younger brother, Tom as the only other partner. It was he who provided the greater part of the clientele. Tom was an unobtrusive man and it was his function to stay at home and keep house. He received me affably and I was ceremoniously introduced to all the other partners who were the in the office. The senior partner was still on vacation.

The firm at that time was called Withers, Benson, Currie and Williams; in its rise upwards it has shed the Benson, the Currie and the Williams. I remember being presented to Benson, Currie and Williams but they operated in a backwater with their own clients and I saw no more of them.

There were two other active partners, a solicitor called Covell, who had come to the firm as an employee and had quite recently been given a partnership, and W. H. C. Rollo. I was assigned to Mr Covell who took me round the three litigating divisions each run by what was then called a managing clerk and would now be dignified as a legal executive. There was a common law department run by Mr Watson, a divorce department run by Mr Emery; an amusing, capable man with a bluff and hearty approach to adultery, and the chancery department under George Baker.

George was a young man of talent with whom I became very friendly although not much interested in his subject. He was fond of John Withers and very grateful to him for his articles. He formed eventually his own firm of George E. Baker in Guildford which is now carried on by Alistair Logan who achieved fame, if he had not won it before, in the case of the Guildford Four. George was to send me several briefs when I was a Junior.

I was assigned first to Mr Covell which meant sitting in his room while he discharged several items of business. Both he and John Withers liked to have someone sitting in the room when they were dictating. John liked to walk up and down the room with his hands under the tails of his morning coat; he interspersed his letters with frequent "my dear sir", or "my dear lady", according to the sex of the recipient which was not infrequently, having regard to the nature of the subject, female rather than male. Covell, on the other hand preferred the impersonal "we" and when he had to refer to himself always said "the writer". The typed letters were copied by some Victorian process into a large letter book. The other documents appertaining to any case were kept in large tin boxes with the name of the client lettered in gold at the top. The boxes stood on a broad shelf five or six feet high which went round the room. The senior partner's room thus discreetly advertised the social status of his clientele. The Duke of Westminster ran through a number of wives and there was a "Constance, Duchess of …" as well as a "Violet, Duchess of …" Mr Rollo, the junior partner, was away cub-hunting, "a great man for the hounds" Mr Emery told me. Bill Rollo turned out to be the partner for whom I did most work and I got to like him very much. He had gone to the Bar but found he was never going to make a living there. He had a good, quick mind but it was not measured enough for the work of an advocate. He told me once how it was that he had come to make the change.

John Withers was one of those men who become extremely devoted to the institutions in which they have played a part, to the point of being convinced that anyone connected with them must be of the superior sort with which they would like to be associated. In the case of Withers, it was Eton and King's College, Cambridge. When the firm of Withers was growing and he decided that he would like to have another partner he put an advertisement in a legal paper in which, after listing the usual qualifications, he put words to the effect that Eton and King's would be preferred. Bill Rollo thought it was worth trying. He was, in fact, just the sort of young partner that the firm needed. He would certainly attract clients from the sort of people in which he and his wife, Lady Kathleen, moved. Withers himself supplied all the traditional marks of the family solicitor – a benevolent appearance, a cautious and shrewd utterance, with the "my dear lady" approach. Bill was brisk, quick on the mark and with a convincing air of getting things moving. He met all sorts of people, not only society people with matrimonial troubles, but financiers, out hunting. One of his big clients was a Belgian financier called Loewenstein[1], embroiled in an unending dispute in the world of artificial silk between British Celanese and Courtauld. He was the sort of litigator who was the lawyer's dream. He stopped litigating only when he fell out of an aeroplane.

With Mr Rollo I found that I had friends in common. He was very friendly with Geoffrey Fry who was one of the Prime Minister's unpaid secretaries and so knew Geoffrey Lloyd. He had a house on Fry's estate at Oare in Wiltshire and it was somewhere round there that he was doing his cub-hunting. It was chiefly through him that I became useful to the firm. The idea of my going there was to see how litigation worked from the solicitor's end, how a case began and was built up and in particular what it cost. The cost of a lawsuit was often one of the heaviest parts of the expenditure, equal to or exceeding the amount at stake. But the barrister knows very little about them and I had been told to make good use of my time in a solicitor's office by seeing how bills of cost were made up and what happened to them when they were taxed by a taxing-master. As I was rightly told, I would be very unlikely to see anything of that sort at the Bar. But Bill Rollo was not

[1] There is a piece about him by H. G. Wells in *Work, Wealth and Happiness of Mankind*, Heineman, London, 1932, p. 468.

interested in costs and, alas, neither was I. But I did quite early find out how a case was, – or at least should be, – prepared for trial.

One of Bill's clients was a Lady B. She was the sort that made divorce suits so profitable. If a wife comes to a solicitor with a complaint against her husband, the solicitor does not have to worry about whether the wife has any money and whether she is likely to win or lose and if she loses how his costs are going to be paid. All he has to worry about are the finances of the unseen husband. Under the common law, a husband is liable for his wife's "necessaries" and these cover a wide field of expenditure. If there are reasonable grounds for thinking that her husband is guilty of adultery, it is "necessary" to go to a lawyer to find out what action should be taken and, if he advises a petition, to have matters set in train accordingly. So the husband ends up by having to pay all the costs win or lose. Sir Max B. was well-known as a rich city man; as soon became obvious, there was no other reason why Lady B. should have married him. She was a bold and brash figure of the sort with whom the most skilful financiers seem so easily to get involved.

She was sure, she said, that Sir Max was being unfaithful to her and that there were places which he was constantly visiting i.e. brothels. Withers were of course in touch with the private detectives who specialised in this sort of work and they were employed to watch Sir Max. They produced detailed reports about "the person in question" and the addresses he visited with evidence to establish that they were brothels. The petition gave all the necessary details.

Sir Max did not take his defence to one of the well-known divorce solicitors. He went to a firm of city solicitors who did a lot of work for insurance companies and who were therefore experienced in the investigation of false claims made under insurance policies. There was also a young barrister Mr V., whom, it was believed, Sir Max had befriended and indeed paid for him to go the Bar. He was not given the junior brief in the case; that went to the son of the President of the Divorce Division who was one of the lesser juniors at the Divorce Bar. They may have taken him on his merits, but they ought to have known that it would do them no good as it certainly did not. The President did hear the case but his son was turned out of the family home and given "no access" (as the divorce term is) during the whole of the suit which lasted for three weeks. Young Mr V. was given the job of working hand in hand with the solicitors to test every item in the detectives' reports.

The lesson I learnt from the B. case was the importance of team work. A case of course starts with the solicitors. They issue the writ and instruct counsel to draft the statement of claim and so on. They do not need to go to him again until the case has been set down for trial. In due course they instruct counsel to advise on evidence. So it is perhaps a year or so later, when counsel comes back to the case.

When the case is 'in the list' counsel is briefed for the trial and from that moment he takes over the general direction. There has never been 'a plan of campaign' directed from the start by the person who has to fight the case. If there is a leader, the consultation a day or two before the trial between the leader and his junior is hardly more than formal. The shape of the case has been determined by the solicitors and by the junior.

A complicated and difficult case needs firm direction from one person throughout. This is what the B. case got through Mr V. So, when the leaders took over it did not matter really who they were. Sir Max had three. One to do the cross-examinations, that was Stuart Bevan; one to provide the eloquence, that was Norman Birkett[1]; the third I had not heard of, he was perhaps an old friend of Sir Max, a former judge in India, called Sir Walter Schwabe.

The case against Sir Max was entirely based on the story of the hired detectives that he visited brothels. On paper it looked very formidable. But when Crockers, the solicitors, with one witness after another, succeeded in showing that, in the majority of the alleged visits, Sir Max could be proved to have been somewhere else, it fell to pieces. I remember Gerald Kelly, who afterwards became President of the Royal Academy, as one of the best witnesses. I do not think the detectives were ever heard of again but whether or not Bill Rollo paid their fees I cannot say; I expect their motto was: "Cash first and performance later".

The judge having dismissed the petition on the verdict of the jury, we paused before proceeding to the cross petition where Sir Max had alleged three co-respondents, one of them well-known. Sir Max was not a vindictive man. An arrangement was made whereby Lady B. admitted adultery with one of the three co-respondents and received a reasonable livelihood as part of the deal. The victim who was saddled with Lady B. was a very nice man, a member of the Savile Club. He was a sort of superior salesman for Rolls Royce cars and took one round on the Riviera which was how he had met Lady B. He embraced his fate happily, telling me that she was the most wonderful woman in the world.

In the other big case which Bill Rollo had, his client was British Celanese, who were at war with Courtaulds in the artificial silk world. The case never came into court. Perhaps it was never intended to be more than just an harassing operation. But it took me abroad, that is to the Continent, the United States was not then "abroad" in the sense of being a place that anyone went to for pleasure. There were various mysterious figures involved in the case and one of then was called "Feeshaire", which I presumed was Fisher but I never saw his name in writing. There was some material at his disposal which had to be collected and put into shape for a purpose which I have now forgotten. Just when I was about to set off to

[1] The great advocate: see also page 138 for his defence of Mrs Hearn.

pack a bag for the night train to Paris I discovered that my passport in the place where you have to put the countries you wish to travel contained only the words the United States of America. The passport was the one I had got in 1925 for my trip to the United States of America and someone – not me – had filled it in with that destination. The sensible thing, of course, is always to put in "all countries in the world" the thing being a mere formality.

I showed this to Bill Rollo. He said that perhaps it would be better to put it right and that he knew a man in the Foreign Office who would at this hour – it was getting on for 6.00 pm – be found in Bucks Club. He thought that I had better abandon the night journey and leave early by plane the next morning when things had been put right; his secretary would arrange the tickets and we would set off for the Club when she got back. When I got them, it appeared to my dismay that the plane left shortly after 6.00 am.

So we met the friend at Bucks Club and had quite a long drink after which he took out his pen, wrote on the passport "and all other countries in the world" and initialled it. I supposed that this was effective but as nobody ever looked at the page I did not know for certain.

Imperial Airways was the name of the concern that then covered Paris, and such other places on the Continent as were within flying distance. There was an imposing array of huts at the edge of a field and I was asked if I would like breakfast on the plane. I walked out to it, quite a distance. It was quite small, perhaps a dozen seats. I could not see where the breakfast would be manufactured. Just after we had taken off I saw a lady come out of the huts with a cardboard box which I suppose contained it. But by then it was too late.

We arrived at Le Bourget after a flight which I greatly enjoyed. Except for three minutes in the air with a friend who took me up to see what it was like, it was the first time I had been in the air. There was a bus on the airport which went to the Place de L'Opera. I had never been in Paris and had no notion of its geography but I supposed that it would be somewhere fairly central from which I could get a taxi to the hotel that Bill had recommended in the Rue de la Paix, the hotel "Vestminstaire". We arrived at the Place de L'Opera and I was directed to where a taxi might be found. Eventually one turned up and I got in, told him where to drive and sat back to contemplate my next step. Almost at once the taxi stopped and man got out and opened the door and spoke very rapidly in French. I was mystified; but it then turned out that the Rue de la Paix began at the Place de L'Opera and that the Westminster was just round the corner. I was so startled that I misread the one franc on the meter and gave the driver ten. He displayed no surprise at being so handsomely remunerated and I went in. It was – and I daresay still is – a delightful and quite luxurious hotel.

I do not now remember anything about my conversations with Mr "Feeshaire" and various other people about which I wrote a report. Everybody seemed satisfied with my week's work in Paris including myself, for I had a good deal of time on my hands and Paris in April is a joy that nobody ever forgets. My cousin Jean – Uncle Jim's eldest daughter who had married a French baron[1], had an apartment in Passy and a lot of friends. I went there often and by way of return took Jean to the opera. We saw Gluck's *Orpheo* and a noted soprano sang *"J'ai perdu mon Eurydice"* but otherwise I found it rather dull.

There was another second cousin in Paris whom I knew well. We had the same music teacher in Aberdeen. I left her at the age of eight when I was sent away to school and to my regret in afterlife gave up trying to play the piano. I had got only as far as the Jolly Farmer. Miss Cran was pioneering a peculiar method designed for young children in which crotchets and quavers were called Ta and Ta-a. It was thought that the shock of translation to the more orthodox terminology would prove too much for me. Ruth[2] stayed on and prospered; she was, at this time, a pupil of Alfred Cortot. We dined very pleasantly at a restaurant called Chez Henri which she thought would not be beyond my means.

---

[1] A delightful man Baron de Boulement who described himself as looking like a Pug dog, and did.

[2] Later Ruth Fermoy, Lady-in-Waiting to the Queen Mother and grandmother of the Princess of Wales.

Chapter VII

PUPILLAGE AND MARSHALLING

TOWARDS the end of my year with Withers and Co. I had to begin thinking about a pupillage in Chambers. What Sir Geoffrey had said, that Withers could make a young man at the Bar, was true if limited to the Divorce Bar. There was indeed a certain amount of work at common law but not much. The junior who did most of it was a hunting friend of Bill Rollo's, Terence O'Connor who was already an M.P. and later to become Solicitor General.

I did not want to go to the Divorce Bar because the work was dull. It gave a man a quick start but finished well below the heights. Stuart Bevan, besides being a very nice man whom I had met, was generally regarded as the Number 2 at the Common Law Bar, after Sir John Simon. There was no junior in his Chambers but Withers, who of course knew him, asked him if he could recommend a suitable pupil-master. Bevan suggested Cartwright Sharp, a junior who had a good but undistinguished common law practice.

It was a very good recommendation – a good ordinary practice was what I needed to see. It was mostly accidents on the road ('running down') or in factories with some breaches of small contracts and so on. There were numerous briefs, small in size and rarely meaning more than a day in court. A year as a pupil was, and still is, the way of starting a practice and it was then the hope, as it still is, that it would lead to a seat in Chambers.

A pupil would look at the briefs as they came in, the most useful ones being those that were sent for 'advice on evidence'. The 'advice on evidence' is the document in which the barrister, when the case is ready for trial, advises what proofs should be obtained from what witnesses. Drafting the advice was very useful training and Sharp was very meticulous about it and a good teacher. He did not take more than two pupils at a time. Some fashionable juniors would take up to half a dozen, put them all in a room together and give them a blessing but little more. Sharp also liked to dictate his opinions to pupils but with me was forced to abandon that because of my illegibility. There was, at that time, no stenographer of any sort employed in the Temple though the clerk had a typewriter for use with one or two fingers. The only fault that I had to find with the Chambers was that they were too *gemutlich*. Sharp liked everyone to lunch together in an inferior restaurant in the Strand called Grooms and if you sought to excuse yourself always made the same joke which was, 'Give her my love'.

Every substantial junior had in his chambers one or two younger men who were employed as his devils. They would read up his briefs, attend the conference with the solicitor and the client and sit with him in court. If he was doing two cases at the same time which might often happen if he was being led by a silk in both, the devil would carry on with the case. In this way the young barrister began to get work from solicitors he met and – if they took a favourable view of him - beginning perhaps with their county court work, being given their smaller briefs if their boss was too busy to handle them and hopefully, when he took silk, inheriting a substantial part of the junior practice. Sharp already had two devils, unpaid of course, but feeding on the scraps and awaiting the inheritance, so I thought it unlikely that when I finished my pupillage I would be invited to stay on, and felt anyway that I could do better.

The Savile Club was not at all a lawyers' club. As I have said it was intended for 'men of letters'. It had also a number of the higher civil servants and it was beginning to get, because of its northerly situation in 'clubland' which put it conveniently near to Harley Street, quite a number of medical men. There were two judges who were members, one of them having been put on the Bench only a year before. This was Mr Justice Charles. He had had a substantial run-of- the-mill practice at common law. He was quite late in his fifties and the general impression was that the Lord Chancellor was rather scraping the barrel when he appointed him. He never pretended to know any law and was slightly contemptuous of any of his brethren who considered legal learning to be a qualification. He was a genial bachelor, fond of company. He had a small flat in St James's and three clubs, which were no more than he needed since he liked to dine out every night, the Athenaeum, the Union (now I think defunct) and the Savile. He was a jovial man, very friendly and kind, but, like many of his brethren, had an exaggerated sense of judicial dignity.

A judge sitting in London is addressed as 'My Lord' and in argument was, in my time, treated with excessive deference.

Certainly judges ought not, when discharging their duties, to be treated with familiarity, but the 'if your Lordship pleases' attitude goes further than that. It dates from the days when many persons of consequence were so treated and when persons of high consequence were all addressed as 'M'Lord'. When a judge leaves the court he becomes an ordinary citizen, hailing a taxi or jostling for a place on the bus as the ordinary citizen does. Not so in court. The High Court sits in London and a judge who tries cases elsewhere, than in Middlesex, does so by virtue of a special commission from the Crown. For civil cases it is a commission of *oyer an terminer* (hear and determine) and in crime a commission of *general gaol delivery*. An accused who is given bail (which until this century was rare) becomes a prisoner when he surrenders to his bail and enters the dock.

The commission, which is read out by the Clerk of Assize at the beginning of the proceedings, names a long list of dignitaries as commissioners empowering 'you or any two of you' to try crime in the county. The Clerk of Assize is always named in the commission so as to fulfil the requirement of 'any two of you'. He sits below the judge and is ready with practical advice if needed.

It is by virtue of his place on the commission that the judge presides at a trial. As one who holds the Queen's commission he claims to be treated as the Queen herself or at least as the royal representative. If the claim is well founded then as Chief Justice Goddard, who did not care for the flummery, liked to point out, all the commissioners including the Clerk of Assize should be treated as royal representatives. But county society likes royalty and, if it cannot get the real thing, a substitute who has plausible pretensions is welcome.

After I had met the judge several times he said that he was going out on his first circuit, the Northern, in June and invited me to come as his marshal. This was a great piece of good fortune and I readily accepted. A marshal was paid two guineas a day and all found. The Northern Circuit would take nearly two months so that I might expect to come away with £150. This would have been a most useful addition to my reserve fund, which was dwindling if I had not yielded to the temptation to spend too much of it on a small car.

The circuit began at the end of May so that it meant cutting short my pupillage with Sharp. He very kindly said that he had a month free in October (the first two weeks were then still part of the long vacation) and would give me that.

30th May was the day of the General Election which returned the Labour Party to power for the second time. Rab's seat was considered safe – indeed he held it without a break for the next 25 years – but Geoffrey Lloyd was fighting a doubtful constituency. He had done his novitiate in a Labour stronghold in the East End and had moved up the ladder to something better. The Chamberlains who had ruled Birmingham for so long were now having to withdraw from the more doubtful areas. Neville Chamberlain, who had been the member for Ladywood for some time, had found his position in 1924 to be threatened and had decided to move to the safer Tory seat of Edgbaston. Geoffrey was given Ladywood to fight.

I had seen him from time to time in London. He dined regularly at the Carlton Club on Sunday nights and liked to invite a friend. The dinner he chose was, as might be expected, well considered and always the same. We drank champagne throughout. We began with oysters and then roast chicken which had to be cooked in a way that he had carefully explained to the chef; this was one of the advantages that flowed from always having the same dinner. We finished with a fruit salad with some liqueur in it served after a careful explanation to the waiter about having various pips removed before it was brought to the table.

He had asked me if I would come to Ladywood to help. This suited me well for the General Election was a day or two before I would start my period as a marshal and I could just break off in the Temple a fortnight earlier.

Most of my time in Birmingham was spent on a lorry with a loud speaker. This was much easier than street-corner oratory since the loud-speaker could always prevail against the heckler. After the morning's work I would lunch with Geoffrey who had spent the morning in influential canvassing and would give him my report afterwards with the coffee. Geoffrey said it interfered with the digestion to discuss matters of that sort at meals.

On the day of the election I got back to London in time to dine with a friend at the Ritz where they were showing the first election results. It was clear at once that there was a swing to Labour which made it unlikely that Geoffrey would hold the seat. He did not. But he settled down politically in Birmingham and became, in effect, the Birmingham Party boss.

The next morning I went to Euston where my duty as a marshal began. We were travelling that day to Carlisle. I was suitably equipped, though I had to make some advance payments out of my two guineas a day. I had an evening tail coat and dinner jacket and stiff shirt for these were necessities for any young man who lived in London. I had purchased for £10 a set of gold and platinum sleeve-links and waistcoat buttons. I had bought a morning-coat which would be my uniform as a marshal: the striped trousers I had already as part of the barrister's dress. I needed also a top hat and a hat box for it to travel in. I invested in a very expensive real leather hat box to hold two top hats, one black and one grey, and a bowler hat. I have still got it, but when the time came when porters were no longer available it proved too much of an encumbrance to carry about.

There were no problems of that sort at Euston on the morning of 16th June. The judge's clerk, a nice young man called Fred, was in charge of the baggage and of a large truck (with four porters) on which it had all been placed. There were all the judge's robes and many wooden boxes to carry his law books. Mr Justice Charles had only two law books, but he always took the wooden boxes for the sake of appearances. An official – not I believe actually the station-master but someone from his office almost equally grand – was in attendance when the judge arrived. We were then conducted to the reserved compartment in which the judge and I would be seated while the clerk, as would be proper in those undemocratic days, took his way to a reserved seat in the third class. There he would be joined by the judge's cook, the judge's butler and the marshal's man. The other passengers passing to and fro in the corridor must have looked with some envy on the empty seats; the occasional democratic judge would beckon them in.

We were going first to Appleby then to Carlisle and then to Lancaster, the county towns of Westmorland, Cumberland and Lancashire. The Assizes there would take a fortnight in all and then there were two periods of four weeks each in Liverpool and Manchester where the bulk of the work would be done. In each of these places there was a large nineteenth-century house and garden kept permanently as the Judge's Lodgings. In the three smaller towns the High Sheriff was responsible for renting a house for the short period. In each house the domestic staff except for the butler and the cook and the marshal's man was provided by the county.

The train went first to Leeds where it performed the manoeuvre required by the ground plan of Leeds station of going in and backing out. Then it set off on the lovely journey across the Pennines to Carlisle. We were going first to Appleby and since the line did not run through Appleby the train had to be specially stopped at Penrith where we were met by the Under-Sheriff for Cumberland, of course with the station-master in attendance. What happened to our luggage I do not know except that it certainly turned up. We were driven in a car with a Cumberland police escort to the county border where Westmorland and Cumberland meet. There we got out, made our au revoirs to the Under-Sheriff of Cumberland, were greeted by his *confrère* of Westmorland and got into another car with a Westmorland police escort and so arrived at our destination.

Work began on the next morning after breakfast when the High Sheriff arrived at the lodgings with various other dignitaries. The judge, fully robed, received him with the marshal, morning-coated, standing decorously by his side. The High Sheriff began by expressing his thanks to the judge for having excused him from attendance on his arrival in the county. The High Sheriff had written before to enquire whether the judge would consent to be met by the Under-Sheriff. The judge always did consent but not long afterwards it proved unwise for the High Sheriff to take it for granted. One of them who, so it was said, had just returned from Africa where he had been shooting big game and had omitted to make the usual request was fined £500 by Du Parcq, one of the meekest and mildest judges on the Bench. It is frequently meekness and mildness that are aroused in these circumstances.

Then the various other dignitaries were presented – the Mayor, the Chief Constable and so on and the Sheriff's chaplain. The chaplain's presence was required so that he could say 'Amen' when the last words of the sentence were, as they so often were in earlier centuries, 'and may the Lord have mercy on your soul.'

Then we all set off to the Church for the Assize service preceded by the trumpeters (the smaller the town the louder the trumpeters) at a walking pace, the judge and the marshal in a coach if one was available and if not in a car. I was taught at once that the marshal must never sit on the back seat with the judge but always on the jump-seat facing him. The Sheriff's chaplain preached a sermon comparing the justice of the world to divine justice to the disadvantage of the former. Then the procession to the lawcourts was resumed and more trumpeters greeted our arrival at the steps.

The proceedings began with the reading of the Commission. Before the age of the railways the Commission had been read immediately on the arrival of the judge. Until then it had never been known with certainty when the Assize would begin. On the days when the judge might be expected a look-out was kept and when the coach was seen word was hurried back to the local dignitaries who assembled in the market-place. So the Commission began by urging everyone to 'draw near and give your attendance'. It still began that way when the reading was in court though then of course any attempt at drawing near to the judge would have been immediately repelled.

But the Commission was framed in archaisms to which nobody paid any attention. It was a very lengthy document beginning with the names of the Commissioners, the Lord Lieutenant first. When it got to the name of the judge, he raised his three-cornered hat in acknowledgement, replacing it with anxiety on his full-bottomed wig, for if not replaced at the correct angle it might lurch and descend.

After many references to *oyer an terminer* and *general gaol delivery* things got started. The Grand Jury who were sitting in the jury-box had to be sworn in. This was the great moment for the marshal. It was a lengthy oath in majestic prose and he had to learn it by heart. There were many injunctions to secrecy but I have forgotten most of them. 'The King's Counsel and your own ye shall keep secret' was one of them, which has led to the misconception that the common (petty and not grand) juryman is sworn to secrecy about what goes on.

The function of the Grand Jury, abolished four years later, was to examine the bills of indictment and mark each as 'true bill' or 'ignore'. To aid them in this duty they were addressed by the judge who would if necessary tell them what to ignore, but he usually confined his address to general matters relating to the state of crime in the county, congratulating Blankshire on the reduction in burglaries while deploring the increase in carnal knowledge under the age of 16 and so forth. The Grand Jury consisted of the gentlemen of the county whose real business was to attend the High Sheriff's luncheon which usually lasted for the rest of the day. One comical side to the proceedings was the use of some mechanical contraption or instrument, such as a pair of long tongs, whereby the true bills could be conveyed from the hands of the foreman into the hands of the Clerk of Assize, thus averting the risk of a nefarious alteration being made en route.

The opening of the Assize was still in these days, as it had been throughout the eighteenth and nineteenth centuries, a social event for which the gentry gathered in the county town. The High Sheriff gave a large luncheon party to which the judge was not invited. This was a relic of the days when the King's Justices were supplanting the High Sheriff's jurisdiction and social relations were distant. The judge would however accept an invitation to dine with the High Sheriff informally. I do not remember the one in Westmorland, but the Cumberland High Sheriff lived in a delightful house overlooking the Eden. This was my first visit to the Lake District. In Lancaster we were lodged in the Castle, a rather forbidding edifice which housed also, I think, the law courts and maybe the prison.

Mr Justice Charles was not a solitary man by nature. He did not read books and had, in the country, nothing to do. He spent no time either in brooding over the judicial activities of the day or in preparing for those of the morrow. So the time which in London he would have distributed among his three clubs he was ready on circuit to devote entirely to the marshal and to the imbibement of quite a quantity of whisky and soda with which I was expected to keep pace. But he had a kindly eye for my welfare and at the weekend told me to take the day off and go out for a walk on the fells and I spent a happy day in Bowland Forest.

In Liverpool we were joined by a second judge, Mr Justice Macnaghten, and became more ceremonious. The car which the High Sheriff hired to be at the disposal of the judges during the Assize had been replaced by a magnificent Rolls Royce which the Lord-Lieutenant had just presented to the Duchy of Lancaster. It had the arms of the Duchy emblazoned on the panels. Unhappily the High Sheriff and his chaplain occupied the jump seats and the marshals had to go by tram so that they might receive the judges at the foot of the steps to St George's Hall. The car was intended for the use of the judges when in robes; Mr Justice Charles was very critical of one of his brethren who, he said, had taken it instead of one of the lesser cars to the golf course: Mr Justice Charles did not play golf.

Twenty years later when I went to the Liverpool Assizes as a judge, the Rolls Royce was still going strong, creating an 'Is this a record?' situation for a man to travel in the same car first as a marshal and then as a judge.

Macnaghten J. was a nice man with a great fund of legal anecdotage. He was extremely active and had a tennis lawn laid out in the gardens of Newsham House where the judges were lodged; we played most evenings. In later life he became rather garrulous and when he had a point to put to counsel it would often develop into a soliloquy. 'If I were to remind you, Mr Smithers, of the rule in Rylands and Fletcher and ask you to apply it to the argument which you have just concluded you would no doubt seek to distinguish it on the authority of Jones and Jackson. But would you not then be overlooking Thompson and Davidson? I do not suppose you would agree with that but I should then be forced to remind you of a quite recent decision of the Divisional Court in which I played a small part. You will find it reported ...' Thus he rambled on paying no heed to the disclaimers of counsel.

In Liverpool there was much official entertainment. The Lord Mayor, the Bishop, the Dean and so on were all disposed to give dinner parties and had in return to be entertained at the Judge's Lodgings. In this flow of entertainment everyone was placed according to rank which meant that your immediate company around the table was always the same as it had been the evening before. There was always a surplus of gentlemen since the judges' wives, (my judge of course had not got a wife) in those days, never came for more than a weekend in the middle of the Assize. The senior judge at breakfast time would issue a ceremonious invitation. 'I hope, brother,' he would say 'that we may see Lady Macnaghten here at one of our weekends.' To which the junior judge would reply that he had no doubt that she would be delighted to come. Charles told terrible tales of judges' wives who had invited themselves more frequently and some who had even ventured to make suggestions about the household arrangements.

A perpetual problem in Liverpool was created by E. G. Hemmerde who was one of a group of four who were outstanding in the Oxford Union of their time. The others were F. E. Smith (Lord Birkenhead), who became Lord Chancellor at the age of 48; John Simon who, in 1928, was the greatest figure at the Bar and became Foreign Secretary, Chancellor of the Exchequer and Lord Chancellor; Hilaire Belloc, the writer and poet. It was certainly difficult in 1928 to see Hemmerde as one of these. I doubt if he was ever up to the mark but anyway his career had fallen on evil days. He went to the Bar in Liverpool, as did F. E. Smith, but he lived above his means and when in dire straits was rescued by a loan from a sympathetic friend. Many years later when the friend sought to recover the loan, he failed to pay; and when sued pleaded the Statute of Limitations which barred any action for the recovery of a debt unless brought within six years of the date when it was incurred or of any later date on which the indebtedness had been acknowledged. This was not a thing that gentlemen did; it was even worse than pleading the Gaming Act to a gambling debt. There was worse to come. The question whether there had been acknowledgement or not turned out to be a knotty point which Hemmerde took to the House of Lords where he lost it. So the case of Spencer v. Hemmerde (1922) A.C.603 was a matter of talk throughout the legal profession.

At some stage Hemmerde had been made Recorder of Liverpool which gave him an income of £500 a year and enabled him to 'continue his practice at the Bar. This was what he was doing in 1929. In the end he made good and earned the respect of his fellows but at this time his situation was very dicey. As Recorder and the Head of the Liverpool Bar the judges had to decide what notice to take of him. The usual practice was to receive him without fervour. In this Assize the Chairman of the

94

Mersey Docks and Harbour Board wanted to invite the judges on a trip around the harbour with a luncheon on board. Mr Justice Charles as the senior judge was dubious about meeting Hemmerde. The Chairman had to play his trump card which was that Hemmerde and he were at Winchester together. This was not a plea that could be resisted by any public school man, as of course all the judges then were, and Hemmerde came to luncheon.

By the end of July when the circuit finished my financial position seemed very secure. I had lived free for two months and earned about £140 to add to my reserve for the briefless days which lay ahead. Unfortunately I was, as I have said, attracted by the sight in a shop window of a very small car known as the Baby Austin. This one was very special being decked out in red and black so as to look like a ladybird. It was an open car of course, two seats and a boot contained in the red and black tail. I bought it. It cost £115. I met my brother Bill and we drove in it up to Aberdeen for the holidays.

The summer of 1929 was the best that I have ever known; others since have touched it but it is still in my memory the best. The sun shone every day.

My father, inspired perhaps by my Austin Seven, bought, though he did not drive, a second-hand Talbot open tourer and decided to take my younger sister Frances to Ireland, where she spent the rest of her short life. I did not like to leave my new Austin out of this expedition so Frances and I decided that we would go round by the west coast of Scotland and meet my father and my brother Bill with my Austin at Larne. The plan was not entirely successful. We reckoned on doing 20 mph but we made quite insufficient allowance for the state of Scottish roads in 1929. The road south through the pass over Glencoe, now I believe a fine highway, was hardly better than a track. It was of course all hills and dales and 7 hp did not make much speed up the hills. Hurrying the car faster than was prudent I took it off the track and into a ditch, where we had to leave it. We were very lucky to find a delightful fisherman's inn quite near. So we had to leave the car, telephoning the nearest garage to collect it, and take the train to a point where we could join the Talbot.

It was the first time in my life that I had been to Ireland. We crossed by Larne then to Belfast and thence by road to Dublin. We stayed at the Hibernian Hotel and spent several days motoring and walking in the Wicklow hills. I do not remember a day when it rained.

Chapter VIII

FIELD'S CHAMBERS
AND THE ATTORNEY-GENERAL

IT HAD BEEN arranged that I should go back to Sharp's chambers in October 1929, to finish my pupillage. He told me with kindness and regret, that he would not be able to invite me to stay on. This was in accord with the views which I already had on the subject but I had not found anywhere else to go to. I sought again the advice of Stuart Bevan and through his good offices, was offered a seat in a very prestigious set of chambers headed by St John Field who was reckoned to have the best junior practice at the common law Bar. He had inherited it from McCardie who was said to be the first barrister, apart from the Treasury Counsel, to be promoted to the Bench from the junior Bar. He had a great reputation as a lawyer but proved rather wayward as a judge. He had not as a junior made a public reputation, but on the Bench he moved into the public eye as the 'bachelor judge'. (The knowledgeable said that he had for many years kept a mistress.) Experience in this field may have enabled him to make the shrewd enquiries about ladies' underwear in a case which he was then trying. They earned him headlines like *BACHELOR JUDGE WANTS TO KNOW* and also some sarcastic comment from Lord Justice Scrutton in the Court of Appeal when the case got there. This so inflamed McCardie that he announced in his court that, in future, he would not supply to any court of appeal, in which Lord Justice Scrutton was sitting, his notebook of the case. This was not so severe a sanction as it sounds since by this time the judge's notes were generally being supplanted by the transcript taken in shorthand. Perhaps McCardie realised this for he accepted some soothing observations by the Master of the Rolls as concluding the incident.

Field, into whose chambers I moved at the end of October, was a sound barrister who operated behind a facade of pomp. He very rarely spoke in court, always being led by a silk, but he bustled about in the Bear Garden where the masters sit to hear interlocutory summonses. The Chambers were in the Cloisters (they were destroyed in the war) where I was allotted, in return for rather a high rent, a very small room to myself. It was the size of a large cupboard but equipped, as cupboards are not, with a window. There was room for a table and chair, and when the solicitor was accompanied by a client or another member of his firm, another chair could be squeezed in. In any other profession this accommodation might have been deemed rather degrading to a professional man, but few came to see counsel who were not tolerant of the overcrowded conditions in which they operated. I waited for work with little or no prospect of ever seeing any. Field already had two devils who would succeed to his practice; the first of them was Gerald Gardiner, who became the Lord Chancellor in Harold Wilson's government of 1964, and the second was Sylvester Gates. Then there was Richard O'Sullivan, a very learned but not very effective lawyer, with a small practice. Douglas Lowe, an Olympic runner and a man of great charm whom I had known slightly at Cambridge, would inevitably attract the eye of any solicitor looking for someone to brief.

Quite early on I was given one of Field's briefs, I suppose to test me out and see if I was of any use. It was a brief to draft "interrogatories", a subject which I had never encountered in Sharp's chambers. When I told Sharp where I was going, he expressed pleasure saying that Field's practice 'was about the same weight as mine'. In fact they were quite different. If he had said that they brought in about the same amount of money he would have been nearer the mark, though I think that Field must have been earning more. In Sharp's chambers, work was divisible into court work and paper work. The heart of his practice was the running down case that is, as Chief Justice Hewart once described it, 'a collision between two stationary vehicles, each of which was on its right side of the road'. There was nothing at all complicated such as one would find in the commercial court.

What Field's cases were I do not know because I never saw any of them, but they must have been much heavier. The brief that his clerk, Adams, gave me to do was obviously sent to try me out. He was not a pupil-master and had no duty to teach me anything: it was given to me to find out whether, as a new occupant of chambers, I could be of any use to him in his practice and it proved that I would not.

Interrogatories are questions which one side puts to the opponent in writing before the case comes on for trial. There was nothing to be found out about them in the books. I know now that their function is very limited. I think – but I am still not at all sure – that it is to obtain admissions. A defendant is not to be interrogated in order to find out what his defence is which of course is what one would like to know. His defence on the pleadings will consist simply of denials; it is for the plaintiff to prove his case. The object of the interrogatory is to see how far the denial is purely formal and to obtain, if possible, admissions which will avoid the need for calling a witness at the trial. It is not intended to be a cross-examination of the defence conducted in writing.

I never heard what happened to my draft interrogatories; I expect they were put in the waste-paper basket. Field was not a man whose time was to be wasted in teaching the younger members of chambers how to do their work. He took no further notice of me. This is not like circuit where barristers are in the same hotel and dine together in mess. London life is different.

It was a great relief to go off for a few days in November to be formally admitted at the circuit's Grand Day and to hold the dock brief which Mr Justice Charles, if he was as good as his word, would make available to me. I went down with Mervyn Clive and we stayed at the Royal Hotel where the Bar mess was established, a large room being reserved for the purpose. The circuit had its own butler and provided its own wine. The ceremony of admission consisted of no more than that during the dinner a message was brought down by the butler from the Silk presiding that 'the President would like to drink wine with you'. Thereupon we raised our glasses and my membership was confirmed. The next day the dock brief materialised.

What is a dock brief? It is a term that legal aid for all in an Assize court has driven out of currency. It was, for a long time, the only way in which a client could have access to a barrister otherwise than through a solicitor. Its potential popularity was inevitably diminished by the fact that it could be obtained only by a person standing in the dock. Such a person had to have in his possession ready cash to the amount of £1 3s 6d, making one guinea for the barrister and half a crown for his clerk. The time to exercise the right was after he had been arraigned and when he was still standing in the dock; he must already have displayed the cash to the warder who would, if necessary, vouch for its availability.

The judge in reply would ask the prisoner whether he had £1 3s 6d and on his replying in the affirmative would tell him with a wave of the hand that he could brief any one of these gentlemen with wigs on their heads (ladies were not sufficiently noticeable to be included) to act for him. Those barristers who rated their services more highly than the fee offered and were sufficiently familiar with the practice to foresee what would happen had gathered up their gowns and quietly vanished; but for any counsel to disappear obtrusively was bad form and not cricket. The prisoner would then look wildly around and point to the object of his choice. The judge would then ask Mr So-and-so to be good enough to take the case. Counsel for the prosecution would hand to Mr So-and-so his copy of the depositions and Mr So- and-so would ask the judge for 'time to take instructions'. This granted, he would enter the dock from behind and follow the accused downstairs where in a small cell he would advise him what to do. In my case this procedure was modified. The prisoner had already pleaded not guilty and the dock brief had been granted, but the case had not been reached. The adjournment put the counsel selected in a difficulty which had been solved by giving the brief to me.

The prisoner was charged with 'breaking and entering', an offence which, if committed in the dark, was called burglary and if in the daylight, housebreaking. 'Breaking' was the essence of the crime, which was founded on a breach of the peace, but the judges had reduced the proof of breaking almost to a formality by holding that it could be satisfied merely by turning the handle of a door or the lifting of a sash window.

In those days even the smallest bourgeois house had a staff of two servants, a cook and a maid, each having an afternoon off a week and a fortnight's holiday a year: the middle classes were still being pampered in this way in 1929. A single maid was a housemaid or, if she waited at table, was a house-parlourmaid. If there were three in the staff, there would be a housemaid and a parlourmaid (tablemaid in Scotland), but that would be rather grand. All maids wore caps and aprons but from these the cook was exempted.

The story of my case, if it were put into a film, would begin with a shot of the housemaid in cap and apron entering the bedroom on the first floor in the evening to draw the curtains. She was the first witness to be called. She deposed to closing the lower half of the sash window and to turning back the covers on the bed. The next step in the drama was taken by the accused, if indeed it was he, who swarmed up a drainpipe, opened the window and, so it was alleged, stole eight pound notes, identifiable as being new and in a series, from a drawer in the dressing table.

When the theft was discovered the police proceeded in the usual way. They had on their books at least two or three persons who committed this sort of crime (their previous convictions could not of course be mentioned in court) and these were all interviewed. They included my client who, when he was searched, had on him eight pounds in new notes in a series. Asked how he got them, he said that he had found them in a hedge by the roadside and intended to take them to the police station. This was the defence that I was instructed to put forward at the trial.

The judge summed up for a conviction and said, as a sort of coda to his summing up, that if the jury were not satisfied that he was guilty of burglary, nevertheless they must, on his own story convict him of 'stealing by finding'. This seemed rather unsportsmanlike but there it was. The jury retired and after quite some time came back with the verdict of 'stealing by finding'. The judge then said all the proper things. He said that if the prisoner had been found guilty of burglary he would have, with his record, sent him to prison for two years; he could thank his counsel that he had been convicted only of the lesser offence for which he would go to prison for fifteen months.

I returned to London where the prospects were very bleak. It was not merely that I had no briefs; it was that in Field's chambers there was no work for me to do, paid or unpaid. My money was running out and at any moment I might have to face the future without any asset except for the little Austin and the possibility of a miracle. The miracle did happen. It happened in this way.

One of the friends whom I saw from time to time in London was Douglas

Woodruff. He was older than me by about five years. He had been at Oxford and was one of a group including Christopher Hollis and Malcolm Macdonald, all Presidents of the Oxford Union. He was now on *The Times* and was already quite famous for the Fourth Leader – a short and witty comment on current affairs, usually non-political. He was one of those people who have, among other delightful qualities, the habit of keeping their eyes and ears open for anything that might do a good turn to a friend.

So he asked me how I was getting on at the Bar and I gave him a gloomy account. He told me that he shared a flat in Lincoln's Inn with Colin Pearson, a friend who was at Balliol with him. He was now a barrister in Walter Monckton's chambers, a good set to be in, and was doing a lot of work for the new socialist Attorney-General[1]. Pearson was a sincere socialist, though he was not greatly interested in anything except the law, and he had written to Jowitt to welcome him into the Party. As the result he was now prospering. Douglas thought that I would get good advice from him and invited me to come and lunch with them in Lincoln's Inn.

I went to lunch and it was a terrible experience. Douglas was a large and unwieldy person. When once I asked him the question which troubled most young men living in London – what did he do to get exercise? – he replied that he took quite enough exercise getting about. The assistance of food for this purpose depended as he often said on the quantity available rather than the quality. Colin seems to have been just as indifferent. They lived in the utmost squalor served by a woman who produced the uneatable in the unspeakable quantities required. Fortunately after they both got married, all this was changed.

After lunch I had a long and interesting conversation with Colin. He was a Canadian by birth but had been educated at St Paul's School from which he got a scholarship to Balliol where he read law and got, I think, a first. He was not a great advocate but he was a first-class lawyer with an immediate grasp of any point that was put to him. He was also a very nice man with a quiet but confident manner. He explained to me what his job was and I here amplify it so as to make it intelligible to the ordinary reader.

The Attorney-General holds an ancient office dating back to 1461 which, beginning as the King's lawyer, has amplified into the Government's lawyer. He is now in control of all the Government's litigation whether criminal or civil. He is assisted by the Solicitor-General who deputises for him when that is necessary. The two together are known as the Law Officers; they are members of Parliament and speak for the Government.

Notionally the Attorney-General represents the Crown in all litigation and when it is impossible for him to do that in person he nominates counsel who are to take

<hr />

[1] William Jowitt.

his place. He does not by custom appear without a junior and he appoints or nominates who that is to be. There is a distinction between appointment and nomination. Appointments are of junior counsel to act as standing counsel to the various Government departments. The first, and still the chief, of these is the Treasury Solicitor, an office which dates from about 1655, who at one time acted for the Crown in all its litigation. At first he was in charge of all criminal and civil work, but in 1908 the office of Director of Public Prosecutions was created for the criminal side. Since then the major departments, such as the Board of Trade, have legal departments of their own and have also their own solicitor. Likewise they have their own standing counsel appointed by the Attorney-General. For all the rest of Government litigation, the Attorney-General nominates *ad hoc* the counsel whom the solicitor is to instruct.

The Attorney-General is *ex officio* the leader of the Bar; he is not a Government minister. For example, in deciding whether or not to prosecute an individual, he acts on his own and is not responsible to any Government department. He himself does not have any department. In 1929 his offices consisted of a few rooms in the law courts in the Strand. In the course of the centuries the office has been encrusted with various minor duties and to deal with these there were a couple of civil servants. He has, like any other barrister, a clerk whom he appoints himself.

It is in keeping with this that he and the Solicitor- General are paid principally by fees on the briefs that he undertakes for the Crown. Until towards the end of the last century they could take any briefs from any solicitor which did not interfere with their work for the Crown.

The Law Officers do, however, in addition to fees, receive a salary considered sufficient to cover the general advice they give and the opinions on questions submitted by the Treasury Solicitor and others. In 1929 the Attorney-General was paid £7,000 a year and the Solicitor-General £6,000. These figures are higher than the £5,000 which was then the salary of an ordinary Cabinet minister and of an ordinary judge of the High Court. In addition the Attorney-General's brief fees at this time amounted to around £18,000 a year and the Solicitor-General's to about £12,000. The curious can ascertain the exact amount by looking at Whitaker's Almanack for the year. The total would be perhaps £25,000 a year which would be about two-thirds of what a top silk such as William Jowitt would be earning in private practice.

It is questionable how much assistance a leader gets from the junior in the case. The two do not normally work together. Briefs having been delivered to each, they meet shortly before the case begins for a consultation with the solicitor and the client. They do not work together as a team. The leader does not pick his junior and any practice inviting the leader to say who he would like to have as junior or the junior to say who would be the best leader is frowned upon. Thus the busy leader needed someone other than the appointed junior to do the 'donkey work' in the case. He would get some young man in his chambers whom he did not pay to act as a 'devil'. It was a universal practice at the Bar – and one of the reasons why it took so long for a young barrister to make a living – that devils were unpaid. Two of the most distinguished Lords of Appeal in my time had, it was said, been over ten years at the Bar before their annual fees amounted to a living wage. All this has been changed within the last few years.

So the Attorney-General with the volume of work which he handled needed devils and unlike the ordinary barrister he had the patronage with which to reward them. This would most probably take the form of ad hoc nominations. But in Colin Pearson's case, as he told me, a new and large source of patronage had been made available to the Attorney- General. It had its source in the rating system.

The imposition of rates on property is one of the oldest forms of taxation. It was first imposed as a result of the Poor Law of 1601 by which the Justices of the Peace in the counties were empowered to raise money for the relief of the poor in the parish and to raise it by rating the properties in the parish at an annual value and requiring the owners to pay so much in the pound. Once devised, the scheme was used to raise money for other tasks with which the Justices as the local authorities were burdened, such as the upkeep of the highways. This became the way in which local government was financed and continued to be the way until it was replaced by an abortive poll tax in 1990.

It was never really a satisfactory way of raising money to place the whole burden on those who owned property. It became particularly unsatisfactory when the properties, instead of being owned by the landed gentry, became largely industrial. This made it a tax on industry which bore no relation to the profit or loss which the industry was making. The Derating Act was devised by two future Prime Ministers, Mr Churchill, who was then Chancellor of the Exchequer, assisted by Mr Harold Macmillan, then a young MP with the reforming notions which young MPs have. It exempted from liability to rates all factories and farms, thus relieving two industries then in a depressed state.

Apparently a sound and simple idea, until it fell into the hands of the lawyers. How do you define a factory and a farm? By saying that they are places where agricultural and manufacturing processes are carried out. But you cannot draw a straight line between the agricultural and the non-agricultural or between the manufacturing process which creates an article and the process which alters and adapts it. If similar legislation were to be enacted today, quangos would be appointed to settle such questions as these. But in the primitive times of the 1920s it was not considered right to displace the functions of the ordinary courts.

Disputes about rates were decided in the country by the magistrates sitting at Quarter sessions (by this time most of the sessions in the counties had legally qualified chairmen), and in the towns there were the recorders who were barristers. These courts decided the extent of the exemptions from rates, their decisions being subject to a case stated for the High Court.

Access for advocates to these courts was restricted. In the case of the sessions the restriction was not inherently unreasonable. It is necessary for every court of justice that skilled advocacy should be available at a reasonable fee. This can be achieved by having a group of 'steadies' among whom the briefs are divided. In this way the journey to the court and the possible stay overnight can be made worthwhile. It was recognised that there might be exceptional cases calling for more than the local talent. So the rule was that no barrister might appear at sessions unless in addition to the ordinary brief fee he was paid a special fee *and* that there was briefed with him a member of the sessions.

It was essential for the Government to present its case through counsel acquainted with the whole of this new subject and up to date with the authorities which were going to be created. So they had to send counsel 'special'. Colin, whether or not the Attorney-General's devil, would have been the ideal person for this. He had a mind which revelled in detail, and the duller the detail the happier he was with it. He was not much more interested in the broader principles of law than he was in gastronomy. Dreary cases were what he thrived upon. Inevitably by the autumn of 1929 the nominations, which he got to do sessions appeals, meant that he had to spend a good deal of time in the country and this was the reason why another devil was needed.

A short list of candidates was being prepared for interview by the Attorney-General. Colin was among those who had been asked to produce a name. The Lord Chancellor had already produced one and there were other exalted sources so the competition would be stiff. The question which Colin put to me was would I like him to put forward my name and the answer of course was that I would.

Apart from anything else, Jowitt would be a most exciting person to work for. He had taken silk in 1925 and was just emerging from a commercial practice into one which would have placed him among the select few who are in demand as advocates, irrespective of the nature of the case. In the year before I had taken Jack Hamson on a tour of the courts intending, in my role as the town mouse, to point out the great figures of the Bar and to my chagrin had failed to identify him. He was a commanding figure, tall and handsome and with a deep and melodious voice. He had only one minor disadvantage and that was that in his early forties he was beginning to get a little thin on top, but in a wig he looked magnificent. It is sad that the twentieth century has abandoned head-gear for the male. Few bald men make an impressive portrait.

Some months earlier I had appeared at a moot at Gray's Inn at which Jowitt was presiding but he was hardly likely to remember that. A week or so later I was telephoned by Cheeseman, the Attorney-General's clerk, and told to present myself in the Attorney-General's room at the law courts when he would see me after he came out of court. He would not reach any decision until he had seen everyone on the list.

He had already seen, so Colin told me, the Lord Chancellor's nominee and it was a relief to know that he had not, as I expected, been immediately selected.

We had a very brief conversation. He asked for a specimen of my handwriting and wanted to know where I lived in London. The specimen he regarded with disfavour but the answer to his second point was obviously satisfactory. He wanted the first because the practice of the law still relied so much on handwritten notes. He wanted the second because it was necessary that my person should, as it were, be on demand at any hour of the day and a large part of the night. He did not say so at the time but I soon learnt that in fact he lived in Upper Brook Street which was a few minutes walk from the Savile Club across Grosvenor Square. So that certainly could not be more satisfactory. There was some pleasant conversation but not much more was said. I was there as if I was, I thought afterwards, a man who enters the witness box to find counsel making up his mind about him in a few minutes and deciding how he was going to treat him.

As I walked to the door to let myself out I did something that surprised me very much. But I suddenly came to the realisation that this was a crucial moment in my life: ahead there was a better start than I could reasonably have hoped for, an interesting and enjoyable life and above all something to do. Behind, there was what I had to go back to. The unutterable dreariness of having nothing to do. If this failed, I had no other prospect. It could not be very much longer before my money gave out and I should have to find some other way of making a living. This went through my mind with such swiftness and intensity in the short walk between the desk and the door that I did something I could not have imagined myself doing. With my hand on the door handle I turned around and said that I was very keen to get the job. He said very pleasantly that he would let me know.

I think in retrospect that it was probably what did get me the job – that and the fact that I had Colin's recommendation as we would have to work closely together – for it was the sort of job that, as Jowitt would have known, demanded, above all else, keenness and devotion. It was the sort of job in which the servant's time ceased to be his own. The law courts in the day; the House of Commons in the evening, whenever it was sitting, and a weekend whenever wanted. I remember rather vividly looking forward to an evening when I had asked Rosalind Henley to dine at The Ivy, one of the more fashionable restaurants in Soho and afterwards to the theatre to see the latest Noel Coward play – *Private Lives*, I think – and to go on to the Savoy to dance, I rang up at six o' clock in the evening to say it was all off because I would have to go down to the House. The calmness with which she received the news was the first indication I had that she led something more than the usual social life of a young girl who had nothing to do but go to parties. She said simply 'of course' and I daresay turned back to her own real activities[1]. But it was part of the unspoken bargain that whenever I was wanted at any time, whether it was an evening or a weekend, I never so much as mentioned such a thing as a social engagement.

I went back to Chambers and duly reported to Adams that I did not expect any immediate developments. The next morning I had actually something to do. One of Jack Hamson's closest school friends was a man called Dennis Bradley. Jack saw a good deal of him and I became quite friendly. His father was the Bradley of Pope and Bradley, well-known Bond Street tailors.

Dennis rang me up in the morning to ask if I would lunch with him at The Ivy to meet his father. His father had ambitions to be a playwright and his first play had been put on in some small theatre and received very bad notices from the critics. It was, I gathered, a pretty dreadful play about a pacifist. In the first two acts the hero was reviled for his pacifism and in the third it was disclosed that he was a retired V.C. One of the critics had obnoxiously described the dialogue as 'tailor's snippets'; and Mr Bradley wanted to sue for libel. Bradley Junior wished to dissuade him and thought that I might help to do so by describing the horrors of libel litigation. We had an agreeable lunch and were given tickets for the performance before an audience which had clearly all been given their tickets too. He did not bring an action for libel.

When I got back to Chambers I found myself treated as a defaulter by Adams. The first thing a young barrister has to learn, he told me, is that he must never be out of Chambers during working hours except to go to court. I received the rebuke mildly though I might have asked him to describe a working hour at Number 2 The Cloisters. He then told me that when the Attorney-General came out of court that morning he had asked that I should be in his room before he returned.

So this is how I began my career. Years later I met the Lord Chancellor's nominee, of whom I had been so afraid. It was when I sat for the first time in the Judicial Committee of the Privy Council. He was the assistant registrar.

At first things were very quiet. The Attorney-General had just finished at the Old Bailey the case of Hatry, an erring financier upon whom Mr Justice Avory imposed the maximum sentence. He was beginning the cases in the Revenue list, disputes

[1] See page 77.

between the Revenue and the tax payer. They were usually on knotty points of income tax law in which the Law Officer was given a note by his junior on counsel to the Inland Revenue. These were short and good and always written on blue paper. All that was needed was to look out the relevant cases and see that they got into court.

The junior was Reginald Hills. I do not think he did any other work except Revenue on which he was ferociously against the tax payer. I remember one note which ended by saying that admittedly it would mean that if the Crown's contentions were right, the taxpayer would have to pay the tax twice over, but 'I trust' he added 'that the Court of Appeal will pay no attention to a sentimental argument of this sort.'

I took up my abode with Colin in the secretaries' room at the law courts and went back to No. 2 The Cloisters only to do the briefs that I began to get. On most days after court was over the Attorney went down to the House of Commons and either Colin or I went with him. He would hold consultations about his cases in his room down there. There was – and I daresay still is – an annexe off the central lobby in the Houses of Parliament with three rooms, one for the Attorney-General, one for the Solicitor-General and one for the Lord Advocate. So this was a second working place with which I became familiar. Then after dinner, if he was not in the House, there was his study at his house in Upper Brook Street. This was on the south side of the street, the usual Mayfair house of its time. The dining room and the study on the ground floor, the large L-shaped drawing room on the first floor and the bedrooms above. The first time I went there I was shown into the study. The Jowitt's were entertaining a couple of friends to dinner and I was bidden in to drink a glass of port. This became the usual custom when I went to Brook Street. Lesley Jowitt was a charming and attractive woman as everyone who knew her would testify and was from the first as agreeable to me as to everyone else.

A weekend in the country was a more elaborate affair. The Jowitts lived at Budd's Farm, Wittersham, a house which they had enlarged and surrounded with a beautiful garden. It overlooked Romney Marsh, being about five miles from Rye and the sea.

Either Colin or I, usually me, as Colin was much occupied with his de-rating, went down most weekends and nearly always there were other guests. The journey by rail was rather tedious. It meant a change of trains at Ashford and getting out at Appledore on the branchline to Rye and then a drive of four or five miles. It meant also taking down an additional suitcase full of law reports. So the little Austin proved a very sound investment. It also during the week frequently took the Attorney and myself from the law courts to the House of Commons.

Chapter IX

THE FOX CASE

ATTORNEYS-GENERAL do not do much criminal work. They represent the Crown in what may be called state trials which give rise to some issue of public importance. By a long-standing custom one of the two law officers appears for the Crown in cases of murder that is committed by poisoning. Sidney Fox was not a poisoner in the ordinary sense, but the way in which he murdered his mother had many of the difficult features of a poisoning case. He murdered her by strangulation and endeavoured to conceal the murder by starting a fire in her room. Sir Bernard Spilsbury, the pathologist, was the chief witness for the Crown. He always gave his evidence tersely and with such certainty that it seemed impertinent to question what he was saying. I was impressed by his assurance: when counsel for the defence began a question by saying that he supposed that the witness had the experience of hundreds of such cases he replied, 'Thousands.'

Fox was committed for trial to Lewes Assizes, a small country court into which everybody concerned was crowded. Mr Justice Rowlatt was the judge. He was a very able man; the subject on which he was an authority was taxation. He did not waste words and delivered even in the most difficult case a brief judgment *ex tempore*. This was a very sensible thing to do since Inland Revenue cases rarely stopped at the court of first instance. Since the final decision would be given either in the House of Lords or in the Court of Appeal, Mr Justice Rowlatt saw no reason to supply these august bodies with a lengthy discourse; he gave them instead a brief and lucid account of the points in issue, told them of his opinion and left it at that. Surprisingly often his opinion was accepted. He had a rather nervous mannerism of ending significant sentences with a little 'Hee, hee'. This no doubt was relaxing in a Revenue case, but it was out of place in a trial for murder.

The trial was fixed for 12th March 1930. Budd's Farm in East Kent was about thirty miles away. The Attorney conceived the idea that a pleasant drive on an early spring morning would make a good start to it. Jowitt always liked to have Colin or myself in court beside or behind him in important cases, since we knew his ways and knew just when and what to provide him with as the occasion arose.

I went down to Budd's the night before. But during the night of the 11th/12th March there was a very heavy fall of snow and the Attorney, who always expected the worst to happen on such occasions, took a gloomy view of our prospects of arriving at Lewes in time for the trial. We started half an hour earlier than planned and just before we left he called to the butler to put his top boots in the back of the car in case we had to walk.

Sidney Fox was born in January 1899. His mother was a handsome woman and he liked to believe that illegitimately he was of noble birth – he was the fourth son of a railway signalman. He first came to the notice of the police at the age of eleven when, in the summary way in which petty crime was handled in those days, he was birched for the theft of fifteen shillings. After that he spent three years as a houseboy in a distinguished family living in Manchester Square. He was a good-looking boy with pleasing ways and it was not long before a guardsman led him into homosexuality. His three years in the servants' hall taught him the way in which the upper class live and enabled him thereafter to pose successfully as one of them who had fallen on bad times.

The three years ended with his discharge for stealing the savings of an elderly housemaid. But he was not prosecuted for that. Nor for the next offence, when he was given the alternative, the 1914 war having started, of joining the army. In between he got some employment in a bank where he seems to have formed the habit of forging cheques which he found useful in afterlife. It was for a forged cheque that he received his first sentence of three months' imprisonment. After that his life followed the usual criminal pattern of a period in – sentences usually of around twelve months - and a period out of prison.

Between his imprisonments, Fox usually joined his mother. She had long since parted with her husband. Of her three older sons, one was killed in the War and another died in an accident in 1915. The third led a respectable life which would not have suited either Sidney or his mother. Unlike Sidney he had not shown, or pretended to show, any affection for her. In her last will which was made as a part of the murder plot, she retaliated in the fashion of the period by leaving him: 'one farthing and the sincere hope that he will never want his mother'. All that is known about that time is that the two of them were very successful in cheating one hotel after another. When Sidney was in prison she took jobs as a cook or a charwoman.

Between 1925 and 1928 Fox enjoyed his longest period of freedom. Towards the end of it in 1927, Mrs Fox struck up a friendship with a middle-aged Australian lady, Mrs Morse, and went to live with her in her flat in Southsea. She was the wife of a captain in the merchant services who was at that time serving in the Far East. Fox joined them and from this apparently respectable base obtained a job with an insurance company which paid him a small salary and gave him the inspiration for a new idea. He made himself so attractive and attentive to Mrs Morse that she fell in love with him. He induced her to take out a policy for £3,000 upon her life and then to make a will in his favour. Having the entry to her bedroom he discovered behind a chest of drawers a gas tap. Apparently it had been left there when the flat was converted to electricity and not disconnected. One night Mrs Morse woke up to find the room full of gas. She managed to crawl out of bed, fling open a window and give the alarm. Soon after this she discovered that a locked drawer in her room had been forced open and some jewellery taken from it. One or other or both of these events alarmed her sufficiently to cause her to give up the flat and return to Australia.

But she left behind her a complaint with the police about the theft. It was traced to Fox and he was given his last sentence of imprisonment for fifteen months. During his time in prison Mrs Fox was admitted to the workhouse in Portsmouth as an indigent person and then moved to hospital because of the state of her health.

When Fox came out of prison in March 1929 he took his mother away from hospital and resumed the pattern of his life in one hotel after another. He resumed also the pattern which he had unsuccessfully employed in the case of Mrs Morse. On 21st April, Mrs Fox made a will in which she left everything to Sidney. Nine days later Sidney took out the first of several accident policies on his mother's life. They resumed their peripatetic hotel life for it was always necessary to move on before the time came for payment of the bill. Three days seems to have been as long as it was safe to stay at the County Hotel, Canterbury, from which they moved on 15th October to the Hotel Metropole in Margate. It is at this point that the evidence for the prosecution begins. For little or nothing of the story was admissible under the rules of evidence.

It was not long after we had arrived safely in Lewes, without the Attorney-General having need of his snowboots, before he was opening the case for the prosecution.

At the trial the Attorney-General led Sir Henry Curtis-Bennett K.C. who was, since the death of Marshall Hall, the best known silk at the criminal bar; and as his junior he had St John Hutchinson, his closest friend from their school days onwards and now one of the busiest juniors at the criminal bar. For the defence there appeared Mr J. D. Cassels K.C., M.P. and his juniors, Mr S. T. T. James and Mr C. Pensotti. Cassels was a Conservative member of Parliament for a London constituency. He was not a lawyer and did not pretend to be; he was a good jury advocate. He took an occasion in the robing room to mention to the Attorney that he would like to go on the High Court Bench. But he had to wait for another nine years and the return of the Conservative Party to power before he achieved that. He was a witty after dinner speaker.

Opening the case to the jury the Attorney began the story with the arrival of the pair, Fox and his mother, at the Hotel Metropole in Margate on 16th October. They were, he said in 'desperate financial straits'. They had left their Canterbury hotel in their usual manner by paying £2 towards a bill of £4 16s together with assurances which the hotel could either like or lump. They paid 4s 6d of a bill of 14s 6d for a night in Dover. They arrived in Margate with only a brown paper parcel for their luggage.

They arrived also with the air of assurance which always seemed to work. They gave the impression of an unpremeditated stop. They only wanted accommodation for the night Fox said, two single rooms with communicating doors, and their luggage had been 'sent on'. Fox made his usual pantomime with an envelope which he wanted to be put in the safe; it gave the impression of a man with some wealth somewhere. Fox enlisted the interest and sympathy of the lady receptionist by telling her that he and his mother had just come from visiting the graves of his three brothers who had been killed in the War.

The next morning, when he was presented with the bill for the night, Fox asked if they might stay on; they had met friends in the neighbourhood, he said. On that day or the day after Fox went to Ramsgate where at Messrs Pickfords, for the price of 2s, he obtained an insurance policy for £1,000 in the event of his mother's death by 'external, accidental means'. In the evening he asked the hotel manager to give him the name of reliable local solicitors as he had some insurance business to transact. He was given the name of a firm; he never went near them, but it all helped to create the right impression.

Then on Sunday 20th October he told the hotel manager that his mother appeared to be in a faint. The manager was much concerned. A doctor was sent for and it turned out not to be anything very much. But in the meanwhile the manager had expressed his concern, observed that their rooms had no fires and suggested they might like to exchange them for rooms 66 and 67 which had a communicating door and in room 66, a gas fire. The doctor came and prescribed a simple tonic. Fox showed great concern, bought for his mother a bunch of grapes and gave the chambermaid 7s 6d to look after his mother because he was going to London the next day for an important piece of business which he could not postpone. When he was in London he telephoned twice to enquire how his mother was.

The important piece of business was with the Cornhill Insurance Company where he went to extend the two insurance policies which he held on his mother's life, one for £2,000 and the other for £1,000, payable on his mother's death 'by violent, visible, external means'. The extensions were until midnight on Wednesday 23rd October. He arrived back at the Hotel Metropole late on Tuesday evening. It left him with something a little over twenty-four hours in which to murder his mother.

On the next day Mrs Fox stayed in her room until the evening when it was time for dinner. The two of them dined together, Mrs Fox eating well and drinking half a pint of beer. Then he took her back to her room and went out to buy for her half a bottle of port; it cost 3s. There were still a few hours left before the insurance expired.

There were three commercial travellers staying at the hotel. They said that at twenty minutes before midnight Fox, wearing only his shirt, came running down calling out: 'Fire, Fire!' Then he ran back, followed by the travellers, to room 67 which was his. It was full of smoke and the communicating door was shut. He pointed to the door and said: 'My mother is in there'. It was Mr Hopkins, the traveller, who opened the door, found the room dense and black with smoke, went in on his hands and knees to the bed and dragged Mrs Fox out. The doctor was sent for and found her to be dead.

Doctor Nichol broke the news to Fox that his mother was dead and that there would have to be an inquest. Fox asked to see the body; he stayed with it for a few minutes and then came out with his eyes full of tears. The management gave him another room in which to sleep and the doctor gave him an injection of morphine.

When he woke, he told his story to Inspector Palmer of the Margate Police. He introduced it with an account of their visit to the graves of the brothers killed in the War. Then he described how he had lit the gas fire for her, left her in bed and gone downstairs for a drink. He returned to his room at about a quarter to ten and went to sleep. He was aroused at half past eleven by what he thought was a window rattling and noticed a smell of fire. He tried to get into his mother's room but was beaten back by the smoke.

The inquest was held on 24th October and a verdict of accidental death returned. She was buried on the 29th.

By the morning after the murder, Fox was himself again and was talking about his plans. His mother, he said, had recently bought a house in Lyndhurst called End View. They had been abroad while it was being redecorated and the furniture from their house at Norwich moved in. His father, he said, who had died in 1913, had been the proprietor of Fox's flourmills. But his mother had a good income and he had never had to work.

That day Mr Harding, the manager of the Metropole Hotel, had a telephone message from the Royal Pavilion Hotel, Folkestone, saying that Fox had been there and had left without paying his bill. Mr Harding reported this to the police and they told him to charge Fox with obtaining food and accommodation under false pretences. This was done on 3rd November and enabled Fox to be held on a charge of fraud.

The charge of fraud, if not the rumours that preceded it, had alarmed the insurance companies who sent down a former police officer to Margate to make enquiries. Then on 7th November the local police called in Scotland Yard and on 9th November Mrs Fox was exhumed. The police took two months to prepare their case and it was not until 9 January 1930 that Fox was charged with murder. On the following day, just to keep things in order, the Grand Jury returned a true bill[1] on the fraud charges.

Five weeks later he was committed for trial for murder and on 12 March, the day of our car ride in the early morning to Lewes, the Attorney-General opened the case for the prosecution outlining the facts on which the prosecution relied. The circumstantial evidence was very strong. The murder was planned, the Attorney-General contended in his opening speech, on or before 1 May 1929. That was the day on which the first policy was taken out on the life of Mrs Fox. From then until her death there were one hundred and seventy six days. The series of policies covered one hundred and sixty-seven of them. The joint income of mother and son during the one hundred and seventy-six days was £22 10s. Just over £10 of this was spent on premiums 'not for an ordinary policy but for an accident policy which covered, and covered only, death from injuries by violent, external visible means.'

When the last of the policies had hardly more than an hour to run Fox could have entered room 66 by the communicating door. His mother, after drinking the port which he had provided, was sleeping drowsily. He put his hand upon her neck, with the other hand pressed the pillow down on her face and thus brought her life to an end. He then started a fire so as to make it appear that the fire was the cause of her death.

The case for the defence was of course that she met her death accidentally in the fire. The Crown might, I suppose, have invited the jury to accept that in some way or another Fox had started the fire in which she was suffocated. The difficulty about this as a planned murder was that the plan supposed that the old lady would sit motionless and surrounded by fumes. Was there any evidence of anything that could have made her so inert?

The Crown had called in Sir Bernard Spilsbury, the chief pathologist and the most renowned in his profession, to see if he could find any sign that would account for her accepting her fate so passively. He did better than that. He claimed to have found evidence that showed that she was murdered before the fire began and that the purpose of the fire was to destroy the evidence of the murder and to create the scene of the accidental death which would support the claim under the policies.

Sir Bernard's examination disclosed a bruise at the back of the larynx, the size of half a crown, which could only have been caused by violence such as strangulation. He found also some small marks on the epiglottis which were very characteristic of death from strangulation. He found in the body no evidence of smoke: if the fire had been started before her death she would have breathed in some smoke.

This was the central point of the trial. The principal medical witness for the

[1] See page 92.

defence was Sydney Smith, Regius Professor of Forensic Medicine in Edinburgh. His explanation of the bruise on which Sir Bernard relied was that it might well have been 'a patch of discolouration from post-mortem staining or putrefaction.' He said that the distinction was difficult to make by the naked eye and after putrefaction had occurred, often impossible. As for the bruise on the epiglottis, it was a spot of haemorrhage of the size of a pin point such as might be found on five out of six cases of natural death.

I doubt whether the medical evidence by itself would have been sufficient to justify a conviction. But the other evidence of murder was such as a jury could easily understand though it could not explain just how the murder was committed. This was what the Spilsbury evidence did.

The defence was led by Mr J. D. Cassells K.C. The summing up was brief and so neutral as to be almost a summing up for the defence. But the jury after an interval of ninety minutes convicted.

The case had three unusual points. It was probably the only case of matricide in the twentieth century. Fox is the only murderer never to have appealed against a death sentence and he is also the only person ever to have been served, while he was in the death cell, with a petition citing him as co-respondent.

As will have been inferred, my contribution to the case was not outstanding. Indeed it might be confined to the exhibition of an epiglottis. We were all staying at a hotel in Brighton where the Attorney-General had taken a suite. I came back into it on one occasion and found the Attorney and Sir Henry and St John Hutchinson debating the issue of how the strangling hand could have reached the epiglottis. He was trying to demonstrate it on the body of Sir Henry who was lying prone on the bed. But Sir Henry was a large man with an abundance of flesh beneath which the Attorney could not find the epiglottis. Hutchy's epiglottis proved no more accessible and it was mine that was selected for the demonstration. But what it demonstrated I cannot now remember.

Chapter X

THE MINT AND CIRCUIT WORK: THE R101

AN EARLY addition to my fortunes and finances came when I was appointed counsel to the Mint at the Old Bailey. There were six barristers at the Old Bailey, usually known as the Treasury Counsel, appointed by the Attorney-General to prosecute in the cases prepared by the Director. There were two other standing counsel at the Old Bailey, one for the Post Office and the other for the Mint. The six Treasury Counsel had their own quarters. The Post Office and the Mint shared a room on the floor above the four courts, – number 1 for the judge assigned by the Chief Justice, number 2 for the Recorder, number 3 for the Common Serjeant and number 4 for the Commissioner. The Commissioner was the judge of the Mayors and City of London court, a civil court with very little work to do so that its judge sat most of the time as Commissioner at the Old Bailey. The Central Criminal Court, commonly known as the Old Bailey, was a court of Sessions sitting at the beginning of each month, but the Sessions were already on the way to becoming continuous.

Early in 1930 there was a vacancy in the Treasury Counsel to which the Attorney-General appointed Laurie Byrne the Counsel for the Mint (later Mr Justice Byrne). To the vacancy at the Mint he appointed me.

The Post Office cases are usually prosecutions of a postman for stealing postal orders of paper money from the letters which he delivered by hand on the rounds which he made on foot or by bicycle. They were heard in the Recorder's court on the first day of the Session.

Prosecutions by the Mint were for counterfeiting, defacing or impairing the gold and silver coinage manufactured by the Mint. Defacing meant any interference with the reproduced head of the monarch who had issued the coin. This, I suppose, was what gave the offence the abhorrence with which the judges of the time regarded it. In the *Archbold* of the year in which I was appointed many pages are devoted to it in the section which deals with offences against the Crown and government, religion and public worship, public peace, public trade and public morals. Twenty-five pages of the close print in *Archbold* are devoted to statutes from 1832 onwards, the year in which a coinage offence ceased to be high treason. The penalty under an act of 1861 for counterfeiting gold or silver coin was still penal servitude for life; for pennies and copper coin, as was only proper, the sentence could not exceed seven years. Its importance had inevitably declined by the substitution of Treasury notes for the sovereign and the half sovereign and was constantly being diminished by the inflation of the currency. Indeed, by 1930 the main outlet for the exploitation of this wickedness was in the automatic machines which sold packets of cigarettes; there the main concern was the manufacture of discs of the correct weight, the points of resemblance to the monarch being no more refined than was necessary to make a glimpse of the disc as it passed from hand to machine resemble a coin. But many of the old practitioners still clung to the more artistic representations which could be used over the counter in shops. Anyway in the thirties there was enough counterfeiting to produce three or four cases at each Session at the Old Bailey.

It was a great convenience, usually enjoyed by counsel much more eminent than myself, to share a room at the Old Bailey particularly since it had its own telephone, a contraption fixed to the wall to suit persons of medium height such as myself and Forster-Boulton. Forster-Boulton had enjoyed his position as counsel for the Post Office for many years; he had no other practice. There were legendary tales as to how he had acquired the post. After passing them through the sieve of the many conversations I had with him I think it was something like what follows.

At the beginning of the century he was in practice in a small way, but his chief interest was in politics where he was a member of the Liberal Party. He was fighting a not very winnable seat in the election of 1906 when the Party was swept into power with all its flotsam and jetsam in the great victory of that year. No one was more taken aback than Forster-Boulton himself. In those days M.P.s were paid no salary. How was he going to live, let alone pay his constituency expenses? He turned to the party whips, using all the eloquence which he had never had much practice in discharging at the Bar and also, I rather think, a not deeply concealed threat. If nothing could be done for him, then he would have to resign his seat. This would mean a by-election. Nothing could be more unpleasing to a victorious party unexpectedly swept into power than the prospect of a by-election at which the victor might well be abruptly unseated.

However this may be, it seems that appeals were made to the Attorney-General as the head of Forster Boulton's profession to "do something for him" and thus he achieved the income necessary to keep him afloat until the next election in 1910 which he inevitably lost, as did many other Liberals.

A quarter of a century later, when I joined him at the Old Bailey, things were not going well with him. They were going worse than perhaps he realised. The Director would no longer entrust him with a case that was going to be fought; the Attorney-General accepted the necessity of appointing one of the Treasury counsel to lead him. Of course the majority of Post Office cases were pleas. But they all came on together one after the other on the first day; and Forster-Boulton began to get them mixed up. It was said indeed that he had a standard opening, which he had memorised, designed to cover all possible versions of the events. I had several conversations with him in which he told me of his fears.

"You" he said, "are fortunate. You're young. If you play your cards rightly," he said, "you may end up a metropolitan magistrate; that is what I would have liked." But he was then 68 and there was no prospect of that. It was suggested that he should be made a K.C. which would automatically cancel his appointments as a junior, but the Attorney gibbed at that. So he gave way and resigned; but lived for another 19 years.

The Common Serjeant at this time was Cecil Whitely K.C.. Before he went on the Bench he had been one of the Treasury counsel at the Old Bailey. He was a bachelor and it was his custom to invite the Treasury counsel to dine with him at Brooke's Club and as he had previously been counsel to the Mint he had included Laurie Byrne in the invitation. So he included me. When I had shaken hands with him on arrival he had looked at me uncomprehendingly and he sought information from Laurie Byrne. It seemed that the absence of my wig emphasised a mass of red hair which had startled him. He was not a great judge but a very pleasant man.

Whitely's predecessor as Common Serjeant had been Sir Henry Dickens, the son of the great novelist, who seemed to model himself on Mr Justice Stareleigh in *Bardell v Pickwick*. It was while I was waiting for a Mint case to come on that I got another dock brief.

When I saw my client he made it clear that he expected to get his £1 3s 6d's worth. He had of course a string of previous convictions so that after a verdict of guilty his imprisonment would be inevitable. He was charged with burglary and his defence was one of mistaken identity.

Unfortunately some of the articles, such as a wallet and a purse with money in it, had been found on his person; he said that they must have been mistakenly identified. It was usual in this situation for counsel to press the suggestion that he should plead guilty with the argument that a plea in mitigation would then be heard more sympathetically by the judge. My client said that he had heard that before and that it had never resulted in any sympathy.

It had been impressed upon me that every Englishman was innocent until he was proved guilty and that every innocent man had the right to have his case, however slender it might seem to counsel, presented to a jury. So I undertook to do the best I could.

I had observed the jury in their box and thought that they might look receptive. In particular there was one lady among the twelve who had caused a mild but friendly commotion when she had been asked if she would mind moving from the front row to the back; the reason for the request being that the enormous hat she was wearing with feathers escaping from it in all directions was said to obscure the view of the juror behind. She had readily assented and became the centre of a small group around her in friendly conversation while waiting for the judge to come in. She seemed to me a lady who was unlikely to think ill of anyone. Conceivably the accused was right in taking a chance.

The prisoner, while stressing his blissful ignorance of everything in the depositions, had said very firmly that he did not wish to give evidence himself because he did not believe in taking oaths. So when the prosecution's case was concluded I said that I was not going to call the accused but wished to address the jury. "Address the jury?" Sir Henry said, "what on earth have you got to say to them?" I indicated as courteously as I could that this was what he was going to find out. But he gave a loud groan. During the course of my brief address he displayed manifest signs of disbelief and finally buried his face in his hands and put his head down on his desk.

His words to the jury after I concluded could hardly be called a summing up. He said little more than that they were to consider their verdict which they could do by the front row turning round and talking to the back row. The process began and it soon appeared that the lady with the hat was at the heart of the discussion. Indeed it was only for brief moments that the hat, bobbing up and down, was discernible among the surrounding heads. She kept it afloat for several minutes before it was finally submerged and a verdict of guilty returned. The minutes were enough to sustain my credit and I have always since then supported the concept of the female juror.

There was not until 1846 any organised system of local courts in England run by lawyers. In each county there were, and had been since medieval times, Justices of the Peace, to deal with local cases and to meet four times a year in quarter sessions. The important work was done by the judges of the High Court who went out three times a year on circuit. There are seven circuits and the Western Circuit was one of them. Each county in the circuit had its Assize town.

On each circuit there were three permanent officials. The man on circuit who mattered most to the young barrister was the clerk of Assize. His function in court was to sit below the judge who was trying crime and act as clerk of the court. His real importance was that he marked with a fee the briefs for the prosecution, most of which came from the police with the officer in charge of the case named as the prosecutor. The police instructed a solicitor and he instructed counsel, usually one of the regular "circuiteers" who had acquired his practice in the usual way by stepping into dead mens' shoes. These did not include cases in which the counsel had been nominated by the Attorney-General but in both classes of case the fee was settled by the clerk of Assize who, at the end of the case, marked the brief accordingly.

In another important respect his duties affected counsel. He made up the list of cases for the day. This was not very important for the counsel who attended one or more Assize towns regularly and was there for the whole Assize. But for one like myself who had a few cases scattered about the circuit it might matter a great deal. If, for example, I had a case at, say, Dorchester and it was not reached on the day when it was in the list it would mean either that I had to spend the night at Dorchester or else go back to London and come down again the next day. The brief fee depended on the size of the case and nothing extra was allowed for contingencies such as that.

The clerk of Assize and the other circuit officers, the clerk of indictments who prepared the indictments in the criminal courts and the associate who sat as clerk of the court in civil cases, were appointed by the judge who was travelling the circuit when the vacancy occurred. They were almost invariably barristers who had failed to make a living and for whom the judge felt that "something ought to be done". The judge, if he was not making a benefaction of this sort, usually promoted the clerk of indictments.

I do not know when Leslie was appointed, but clearly he had been the personal selection of some judge. He was not even a member of the Western Circuit but had belonged, I think, to the Oxford. He was an able man who had failed to attract solicitors with briefs to dispose of. So he was a disappointed man, a waspish man, difficult to keep on the right side of. I began but did not end up there.

Snell, the clerk of indictments, was a nice man of no significance. Robert Seton, the associate, was a benevolent joke, in his sixties.

I joined the circuit without having any local connections because it was the circuit to which Mr Justice Charles belonged. He was "riding" the circuit in the Michaelmas term ("riding" is a term which was still used though coaches and horses had, for over half a century been displaced by the railway) and he had told me that he would see that I got a dock brief. This was the total of my expectations when I was called to the Bar.

At first and for a little time I was in Leslie's good books despite his cantankerous ways. I fell out with him a year or two later at Exeter. Mr Justice Finlay was a very agreeable judge and a very nice man. For some reason he (or perhaps Leslie) decided to open the Exeter Assize on a Saturday. I had one case, a very short one for the defendant was pleading guilty. As it was at the weekend, I thought it was just worthwhile going down to Exeter to do it. The Assize began, as was customary, by taking all the pleas and disposing of them. But when Leslie had taken all the pleas except my case he began to put a jury in the box for the first defended case. The judge had already said that he was not going to sit in the afternoon. So this meant that I would have to go away and come back to Exeter on the Monday when the case might or might not be in the list. The fare from London to Exeter and back was not what it is today but neither were the fees.

Leslie knew perfectly well what he was doing and I thought it was time to make a stand. So I rose and asked the judge whether he would be good enough to take the case of R. v. Blank which was a plea that would take only a very short time and would mean that I would not have to make another journey to Exeter.

Finlay began to say yes, of course, or something like that, when Leslie rose from his seat beneath the judge to expostulate. The judge and he had quite a conversation before the judge said that it was a very exceptional application but that, on this occasion only, he would grant it. Leslie hissed across the table: "Never do that again." But by this time my work on circuit was ceasing to be of the very first importance.

From time to time in my circuit work I made a blunder due to ignorance of the practice. In one case, which was being heard by Finlay, I found that before the magistrates the man from the Director of Public Prosecutions had made an application that a witness should be treated as "hostile". I could find nothing in *Archbold* about hostility and so, hoping for the best, when I got to the vital point, I made the same application. This caused as much commotion as if I had dropped a ton of bricks. I was, of course, familiar with the rule that counsel may not cross-examine his own witness, he may not put leading questions to him nor challenge his answers. A witness is not hostile just because his evidence does not support the other side's case. In practice hostility means that he has changed his story; and the evidence of that is usually a written statement of his evidence which contradicts the evidence he is giving. In a criminal case that usually means that a prosecution witness is retracting something to which he has sworn. So the application for "hostility" must be cautiously approached. Here is an example:

Q: You have just said, Mr Snooks, that you have never been in Brighton and were not there on this day.

A: Yes.

Q: Would you now look at this piece of paper. You will find at the bottom that it is signed.

A: Yes.

Q: Is the signature yours?

A: Yes.

Q: It is, is it not, your deposition in this case made on oath?

A: Yes.

Q: Is it true?

A: No.

Q: My lord, I ask leave to treat the witness as "hostile".

I managed somehow to continue when the commotion had subsided. At the end of the day the judge sent for me and explained to me in the kindest terms what "hostility" was.

There were a number of other things that the young barrister can learn only by watching and observing the way in which an experienced barrister conducts a case. Pupillage is not enough for this. But the Bar is a profession and not a trade. Traders do not usually help each other out, barristers do and do it as a matter of course. I had often to ask for help and I always got it from men much older than myself from whom I was taking what would otherwise have been theirs. The Bar was a profession in which it was difficult to make a start and there was I getting the sort of work for which many had waited for years. But I never had a sour look from anyone.

Circuit life has sustained two changes. The first was the coming of the railways. Before that the judges "rode" the circuit (I expect they usually sat in a coach) right round from beginning to end. The next change in 1945, a minor change, was the intrusion of the divorce judge with the matrimonial list to add to the civil and the criminal; before that divorces were dealt with as part of the civil list. The big change was in the legislation following the Beecham report in the 1960's. This put the county tiers into three classes. The first consisted of the biggest cities, mainly those which were taking two or more judges; the other tiers were visited only if they had something substantial to offer.

This meant that the smaller county towns were no longer visited. In effect it was only the places to which two judges had gone that provided the circuit. This cut out all the smaller county towns. They were often the most pleasant to stay in. In all of them a visitors' book was kept and sometimes the suggestions made were heeded. I once put my name to a series of entries recommending the purchase of a refrigerator. The Marshal, looking back over the past books, had found a series of entries recommending the provision of a bath. It began for a single judge who went first to Wiltshire, Devizes and Salisbury taken alternately as the county towns. He went next to Dorchester in Dorset where Taunton alternated with Wells, then Somerset, then to Bodmin in Cornwall. He was joined by a second judge for the city and county of Bristol, at Exeter for Devon then at Winchester for Hampshire. Winchester would doubtless have been a place for one judge only. Winchester was the only place on the circuit which could be served from London. There were good and fast trains to Bristol but not at the right times.

On 5th October, 1930, just as we were settling down to the beginning of the

Michaelmas term, an event occurred which determined that the future of air travel belonged to the aeroplane and not to the airship.

The largest aeroplane at that time could transport only a small number and travel only a short distance. Many people, including the British Government, foresaw intercontinental travel as something which only the airship would achieve.

The British constructed two airships, numbered R100 and R101, capable of great distances in a single flight. 5th October 1930 was chosen as the day on which the R101 should make a trial flight to India. It was carrying 54 passengers and crew among whom was Lord Thomson, the Secretary of State for Air.

It had got no further than to cross the Channel before it crashed near Beauvais in the north of France. There were only eight survivors, none of them in a position to say exactly how it happened; it seemed that when it was flying in darkness and too low, a downward current of air on its nose forced it to the ground where it burst into flames.

The Government appointed an enquiry to be held by Sir John Simon. It would be opened by the Attorney-General who would be appearing with the Solicitor-General and Treasury counsel.

There was a photograph in *The Illustrated London News* of the enquiry which shows me sitting on the right of the Attorney-General with the Solicitor-General and Wilfrid Lewis, the Treasury junior on his left. By October 1930 my function was well established. I had prepared a note in the way Jowitt liked, every incident noted, all in strict chronological order. If he wanted a document I knew immediately where in the large bundle of papers it was to be found.

It was the first time that I had done a detailed note of the sort that the Attorney-General liked. He did not want, normally, in a case of this sort, opinions or analysis but a straightforward note as I have said in strict chronological order of every event that might be material.

The Attorney was extremely quick at picking up the facts. He could and did open a case simply from the note I had prepared. It was of course a very full note and intended for reading with the papers available as it were, only as exhibits. It could be said of him as it was said of Sir John Simon by some chancery judge, whose name I have forgotten, that he always liked it when Sir John Simon opened a case before him because it enabled him to see which of two entirely fresh minds could pick up the facts more quickly.

The R101 enquiry was held in October 1930 with Sir John Simon presiding. I remember, shortly before the case opened running across Oliver Baldwin. Stanley Baldwin's eldest son was not of his father's persuasion. While his relations with his father were very good, he was an active member of the socialist party. He was a seeker after new ideas, one of which was spiritualism. He told me that he would take me to a seance at which Conan Doyle, who was dead, would tell us all about the R101 and how it crashed having spoken to all the non-survivors. Instead of a simple acceptance, I foolishly told him that that would be very interesting as I now had all the facts at my fingertips. A day or two before the seance he rang me up to say that unfortunately, as I understood it, Conan Doyle would not be able to get back from China in time.

The result of the enquiry was to establish what had happened but not why. It was the end of the airship, no other was constructed, and no one heard anything much more about the R100 or any other airship.

I have mentioned the new Solicitor-General Sir Stafford Cripps. He had taken silk in 1927 and had built up a big practice at the patent Bar. He was the son of Lord Parmoor who had been a minister in the first Labour government; he would have been an obvious choice for Attorney-General in 1929. Perhaps his practice was considered to be too recondite, or it may be that he was thought to be too young, in 1929 he was only just forty and he was still fairly new in silk. The man who was appointed was James Melville, a party stalwart of no great attainments; he was never in good health and it was on his resignation that Stafford was appointed. I never did any work for him as Solicitor General, – he had his own devil – but at the end of the R101 came to know him quite well.

Stafford did not join the National Government but in 1931 went back to the Bar where he soon became accepted as one of the few leaders in any type of case who could obtain the fees he asked. We always remained friends. He had always been a socialist, and in the late thirties moved further and further to the left of his party. Whether he actually accepted Marxism I do not know. He would not have anything to do with rearmament and the popular front against Hitlerism on the ground that the capitalists were not to be trusted with armaments. When Russia was invaded he seemed the ideal man to be sent to Moscow as ambassador; his experience seems to have cured him of Marxism. Also he always remained a fervent and committed Christian.

After the war he became Chancellor of the Exchequer in the Attlee government and earned the name of "Austerity Cripps". His true nature was quite different in his private social life he was easy and amusing. The reference in the *Dictionary of National Biography*[1] to "the public picture" being belied by "the private charm and kindness" hits the nail on the head. Quite how he reconciled his Marxism with his principles I do not know.

Jowitt and he in combination were certainly the two best law officers that I have known and I cannot think of any other combination in history of the same quality. They were both men of high intellectual power and they both lacked any

[1] 1951-60. p. 227.

understanding of pedestrian thought. Jowitt in particular never really understood why he was vilified for his switch from liberalism to labour in 1927 which everyone put down not to conviction but to a desire for office. Of course on paper he was doing the only sensible thing. As a Liberal he had always inclined to the left rather than to the right. The elimination of the Liberal party in the election of 1929 made the choice between the other two parties inevitable for any politician. He was badly needed as Attorney-General by Ramsay MacDonald with whom he had become quite friendly. What could be the point of a parade of doubts and hesitations?[1]

Jowitt and Cripps have another minor claim on history. Besides being the best law officers they were the only two so far as I know to be expelled by the Labour party, Jowitt in 1931 for moving with Ramsay MacDonald to the right and Cripps in 1938 for moving too far to the left.

---

[1] There is an excellent analysis of this in Professor Heuston's *Lives of the Lord Chancellors.*

Chapter XI

THE HEARN CASE

IT WAS SOME time in the winter of 1930-31 that I first heard of the case of Mrs Hearn. She lived with a sister in a part of Trenhorne House in Lewannick, a small village near Launceston in Cornwall. The other part was occupied by a Mrs Pearce who gave some evidence at the trial.

The sister, Minnie Everard, was nine years older than Mrs Hearn and something of an invalid. Mrs Hearn was on friendly terms with a farmer, Mr Thomas, who lived with his wife at Trenhorne Farm, terms friendly enough to cause some gossip but not enough (if she heard the gossip) to disturb Mrs Thomas.

On 18 October 1930 Mr and Mrs Thomas drove Mrs Thomas' mother, Mrs Parsons, who had been staying with them, back to her home. It had been suggested that Mrs Hearn should come with them for the drive and that on the way back they might stop at Bude for tea. In Bude they went to a cafe, Littlejohn's, and Mr Thomas ordered tea and cakes. Then Mrs Hearn produced a packet of sandwiches which she had made with tinned salmon. There was nothing unusual, the waiter said, in customers bringing in food of their own. What was unusual was that one of the sandwiches contained enough arsenic to kill. Mrs Hearn offered them around. It would be natural to offer first to Mrs Thomas and then Mr Thomas and then take one herself. This is probably what happened. Certainly Mrs Thomas took one and Mr Thomas took one or two and Mrs Hearn herself ate one.

On the way home Mrs Thomas became violently ill with severe stomach pains and continuous vomiting. She was a woman in good health who had never suffered like this before. The doctor was summoned and, on being told what she had eaten, concluded that it was some form of food poisoning. The next day she was no better. Mrs Hearn stayed at Trenhorne Farm to help nursing her. The violent sickness continued and there began to develop a tingling in the legs. Mrs Parsons was sent for and took over the nursing from Mrs Hearn. Eventually on 3 November a specialist, Dr Lister, came out from Plymouth. He immediately diagnosed arsenical poisoning and sent Mrs Thomas straight into Plymouth hospital. On 4 November she died. A post-mortem examination showed 0.85 grains of white arsenic in the body. This form of arsenic can be obtained from weedkiller.

Mrs Hearn stayed on at Trenhorne Farm and accompanied Mr Thomas to the funeral at which a Mr Parsons, Mrs Thomas' brother, made some pointed remarks. Undoubtedly, there was gossip concerning Mr Thomas and Mrs Hearn. 'The blame will come heavier on you than me' was one of the things which Mr Thomas was heard to say to Mrs Hearn. Then she wrote a letter to Mr Thomas in which she hinted that she was going to take her life. Mr Thomas gave the letter to the police. They found her coat on the cliffs at Looe and one of her shoes was washed up by the sea.

Evidently the gossip had extended beyond Mrs Thomas, for the police exhumed not only Mrs Thomas but also two other bodies. One was of the sister, Minnie, who had died on 21 July. The other was of Mrs Hearn's aunt who had died in November 1926. All three bodies contained substantial quantities of arsenic. Both women had been nursed by Mrs Hearn and had suffered stomach pains before their deaths. The aunt left Mrs Hearn a small legacy.

Where was Mrs Hearn? Had she really drowned herself?

I remember that I was travelling back to London after doing some case on circuit when I read in the evening paper of 12 January that Mrs Hearn had been found, arrested and charged with murder. The news was splashed in the paper and clearly the trial would be sensational.

Minor crimes are tried summarily by magistrates. Major crimes which are indictable offences are tried by a judge of the High Court and a jury at Assizes. An indictment is normally preceded by an enquiry in the magistrates' court as to whether or not there is a strong *prima facie* case. If the magistrates find that there is, the case will be committed for trial at the Assizes. If they find no case for committal, which is very rare, that is an end of the proceedings.

The proceedings before the magistrates also serve the purpose, if the case proceeds to trial, of informing the accused in detail of all the evidence against him. For the prosecution must call all its witnesses, who are examined and maybe cross-examined by the defence, and the evidence is taken down in writing and forms what is known as the depositions. It is very important to see that all the evidence that is going to be called at the Assizes is called before the magistrates and gets on to the depositions. This task was usually performed by a staff member of the office of the Director of Public Prosecutions.

But it so happened that all the staff were engaged in other cases, except for a Mr Pashley whom the Director did not consider to be quite up to the mark. So he went to see the Attorney-General and asked for counsel to be appointed whom Mr Pashley would instruct. He expected, no doubt, that the Attorney-General would nominate one of the Treasury counsel or a junior of equal experience on the Western Circuit. He must have been very shocked when I was nominated, but he was still in his first year as Director and did not protest.

So Mrs Hearn had not drowned herself. Instead she had gone secretly to Torquay, where under a false name she answered an advertisement for a housekeeper by a Mr Powell, an architect. The press featured the story of the woman who might "help the police with their inquiries". The Daily Mail published her photograph and offered a reward of £500. The photograph was recognised by Mr Powell who informed the police and obtained the reward. He was not a money grabbing man and was sufficiently impressed by Mrs Hearn to use the reward to provide a defence for her. In some way or another, perhaps through an Everard brother in Grimsby, a Mr Walter West, a Grimsby solicitor, was given the money and the task of defending Mrs Hearn. Mr West was a vigorous man and this was a great opportunity. He decided to fight for his client in the committal proceedings where he would conduct the defence himself. This was not very wise. There was not a hope of Mrs Hearn being discharged by the magistrates. He would have done better to reserve the defence and use the committal proceedings for making a few useful points for the defence here and there and save as much as he could of the £500 for the trial. Instead of doing that he made his presence felt by taking a large number of objections, only one of which succeeded.

So, in due course, accompanied by Mr Pashley, I travelled down to Launceston where the committal proceedings began on 24 February 1931. I had never prosecuted in any committal proceedings before. But it was clear that my function was to see that all the evidence necessary to constitute a strong *prima facie* case got on to the depositions and got there in a clear and orderly manner. I had to decide with the valuable assistance of Superintendent Pill, the officer in charge of the case, what witnesses should be called and on what points.

This I succeeded in doing but it was rather like a jigsaw; every piece had to be fitted in. If, for example, the analyst gave evidence that he had examined some internal organ of the deceased and found traces of arsenic therein, the evidence had to detail the process by which the organ had got from the corpse to the analyst and prove every step in the chain. We had to prove that the corpse was indeed the corpse of Mrs Thomas. Then we had to prove that the organ to be examined had been taken from the corpse. Then we had to prove that the analyst who found the arsenic in it was examining the right corpse, even to the point of calling the policemen who conveyed the organ from the corpse to the laboratory of Dr Roche Lynch, the analyst retained by the Crown. He had his laboratory at St Mary's Hospital in Paddington. I visited it as infrequently as possible because of the smell from exhibits past and present.

There was not then, and in the main still is not now, any room for admissions in a criminal case. In a civil case facts are cleared out of the way by obtaining admissions from the defence on every point that they are not prepared to challenge. In a criminal case at that time they had all to be proved by evidence on the depositions, that is, by question and answer taken down in longhand by the clerk to the magistrates, read over to the witness and signed by him.

Great preparations were made for the committal proceedings; they were heard at Launceston by a Bench of eight magistrates presided over fortunately by a very good chairman. They were not held in the small magistrates court. The Town Hall, which could seat 300, was taken over and a raised dais for the magistrates constructed at one end. The hall was always full; *Surging crowds strive for admission* the local press headlined.

Before we began the Crown had to take two decisions which I thought could be taken only by the leader who would conduct the case at the trial. So I had asked for a consultation and Mr Du Parcq KC, later Lord Du Parcq, was nominated. There was evidence for three charges of murder. The first was the murder of the aunt who had died of arsenic poisoning in 1926 after being nursed by Mrs Hearn in whose house she was living. The second was the murder of the sister, Minnie, who died also of arsenic poisoning on 21 July 1930. The third was that of Mrs Thomas who died on 4 November 1930, again of arsenic poisoning. But it had to be conceded that there was arsenic in the soil of Cornwall; so the Crown must prove that no arsenic could have entered the coffins and penetrated the bodies. Dr Roche Lynch was ready to say, in the case of Minnie and Mrs Thomas, who had been recently buried and whose coffins were still intact, that this was so. But in the case of the aunt, buried in 1926, the coffin had crumbled and Dr Roche Lynch admitted the possibility that the arsenic might have come from the soil.

The third point was that the sister Minnie, who had been poisoned, the analyst said, for over seven months, kept a diary in which she recorded the symptoms of her disease. The evidence of the two doctors who attended her was vague. Neither of them right up to the end had diagnosed arsenic. Minnie was an invalid who suffered from digestive disorders and the doctors had taken no particular note of her symptoms; would the diary be admissible in evidence? Under the normal rules it would not. The strict rules of proof required that the author of the document should be called to testify to what he had observed, though it would be permissible for him to look at the document 'to refresh his memory'. This meant that if the author was dead there could be no proof. There were, however, a number of exceptions established to this rule.

It is true that neither of these questions could be finally decided until the trial. But it was very undesirable that, in a case which would be voluminously reported, evidence prejudicial to the defence should be given and published at the committal proceedings only to be excluded by the trial judge.

There were two points on which he was asked to make the decision. The first was whether any charge should be made in respect of the aunt's death. There were two other murders and if the evidence stopped there it would be pointless to add a doubtful third. But it did not stop there. On 29 July, 1926 Mrs Hearn bought from Shuker and Reed, a shop in Launceston, a pound tin of weedkiller which contained 70% arsenic. Certainly the small garden at Trenhorne House was something of a jungle on which weedkiller could have been used, but by 1930 there was no sign that any of it had been used in the garden. It was sometime later in the year 1926 that the aunt died. The tin of weedkiller was found by the police in a garden shed after Mrs Thomas' death. Incidentally Shuker seems to have been an emporium supplying a variety of goods. For on 4 August 1930 Mrs Hearn bought from them, for two shillings, a one pound tin of salmon.

This was the only purchase of arsenic that was traced to Mrs Hearn. If the case of the aunt was dropped, it would mean that three years passed between the purchase of the weed killer and any evidence of its use. Accepting that a charge of murder of the aunt would be likely to fail, the fact of a death following so closely on the purchase would at the least establish the connection. Du Parcq, however, decided that it would not be right to make a charge of murder which the prosecution expected to fail simply so as to strengthen the proof of another murder.

Two or more charges of murder can be made at the same time before the magistrates and heard together in deciding whether there is a case for a jury to consider. But when the case got to the Assizes for trial, an old rule forbade a charge of more than one murder in an indictment. If the aunt's case was dropped and Minnie's retained, the two murders would have to be put in two separate indictments. But it had also been established by the common law that there were cases in which evidence could be given of murders that were not included in the indictment.

The classic case establishing this was popularly known as the Brides in the Bath. The wife of the accused, a Mr Smith, was shortly after the marriage found drowned in the bath. Mr Smith then moved to another part of the country where he married and where the same thing happened. In each case, he had the wife make out a will in his favour. Altogether there were more than half a dozen similar cases. Mr Smith was put on trial and evidence was given of the similar deaths. Although the Crown was unable to prove that Mr Smith had caused the deaths or even to suggest a convincing theory of how they had happened, the court laid down the general rule that evidence of similar deaths might be given to rebut a defence of accident or mistake. In the Hearn case Du Parcq advised that the Crown should tender it and the judge admitted it.

The second point was the admissibility of the diary. The defence opposed it as hearsay evidence. It is generally true that the only way of proving a document is by calling the maker who can be questioned about its truth or untruth. From this it would follow that if the writer is dead, the document cannot be admitted in evidence at all. Common law has established various exceptions to the general rule, for example in the case of dying declarations, but the diary did not fall within any of them. But a doctor is always permitted to give evidence of symptoms which an invalid has given to him. Is not written evidence in a diary just as good? But the judge at the trial disallowed it. In such cases the judge does not concern himself solely with the law. The Court of Appeal may quash any conviction in which evidence has been wrongly admitted; so if it is of little value as well as doubtful a judge will very likely rule against it.

The trial opened on 16 June. The two indictments, one for the murder of Maria (Minnie) Everard, and the second for the murder of Mrs Thomas, were put to the accused in the absence of the jury. To both of these, Mrs Hearn pleaded not guilty and the Crown elected to proceed first on the murder of Mrs Thomas.

Mr Du Parcq opened the case for the Crown. Mrs Hearn and her sister, counsel said, came to live at Trenhorne House in 1925. They soon became on friendly terms with Mr and Mrs Thomas who lived at Trenhorne Farm. It was clear that Mrs Hearn had not much money. In December 1928 she borrowed £30 from Mr Thomas and gave him an acknowledgement in writing. Then followed the story of the tea party at Bude and its consequences.

Between 7.00 and 7.15 Mrs Thomas began to be sick and she sat on the side of the road for about half an hour. Then they went on to Launceston where Mr Thomas parked the car and went away to do some business. When he came back he found that his wife had been sick again. They left Launceston about 9 o'clock and drove to Trenhorne Farm where Mr Thomas sent for the doctor. He came about 9.30 and when told that Mrs Thomas had eaten fish sandwiches, he diagnosed food poisoning and prescribed a medicine called Kaolin. Mrs Thomas got no better and the same symptoms recurred. Mrs Hearn had stayed on at Trenhorne Farm and done the cooking; on that day Mrs Thomas' mother, Mrs Parsons, arrived and took over the cooking and nursing. The invalid did not improve and on 3 November the doctor concluded that this was not a case of food poisoning. He called in Dr Lister, a consultant from Plymouth, who diagnosed arsenical poisoning, and ordered her to be taken at once to Plymouth hospital. This was at 1.30 am on 4 November and at 9.35 am in the hospital she died.

There was a post-mortem in which the analyst found 0.85 grains of white arsenic. Mr Thomas told Mrs Hearn about the post-mortem and, according to her, said, 'They are going to send some organs for analysis and they will find out what it is. They will blame one of us. The blame will come heavier on you than me.' It was after this conversation that she wrote the 'suicide' letter and that her coat was found on the cliffs at Looe; it seemed she had, however, taken the precaution of wearing a woollen jacket underneath the coat. She went to Torquay where she answered an advertisement by Mr Powell for a general servant, giving her name as Mrs Faithful.

There followed the legal argument about the admissibility of the diary and of the evidence relating to Minnie Everard's death. The judge ruled in favour of the defence on the first point and excluded the diary. He admitted evidence of Minnie Everard's death and Mr Du Parcq then proceeded to describe that evidence. The Crown's case was, he said, based upon the analysis of Dr Roche Lynch that Minnie, who died on 21 July 1930, had been poisoned by Mrs Hearn with small doses of arsenic over seven months before her death.

After this he called the evidence for the prosecution. There were no surprises in the cross-examination.

Mrs Hearn was the only witness for the defence. Her manner was perfect. She would have been a marvellous witness if she had had anything to say. But how did the arsenic, which it was proved she had bought, get into the sandwich? And how did the arsenic get into the food which for five months she had cooked for her sister? This was not the sort of brutal cross-examination that Mr Du Parcq knew how to do effectively; he was a 'let the facts speak for themselves' man. Mrs Hearn got away with a look of baffled innocence.

Then came the final speeches. Mr Du Parcq spoke first to close the case for the Crown. Mr Birkett (Norman Birkett, the famous advocate) had not made an opening speech for the defence and had called only his client and was therefore entitled to the last word in reply, the last word, that is, except for the judge's summing up. Du Parcq had not said more than a few sentences before his voice faltered. He said something to me which I did not understand and then collapsed in a faint. Birkett sprang to his assistance and he was able to walk slowly to the judge's lodgings where he was given a bed to lie down on and rest. Dr Roche Lynch, who was somewhere near, was sent for and said apparently that there was nothing serious and that he would be all right after a few hours; he may have had something for breakfast that disagreed with him. Naturally nobody mentioned food poisoning.

The judge, who had adjourned the court and was at the lodgings, sent for me, said that he thought Du Parcq would be all right after a little while and able to continue with his speech, but that if he was not then I would have to make it. What a pity, I could not help thinking, that we were not appearing for the defence. The junior who rushed into the breach and secured an acquittal would have achieved eternal fame. But no one has ever achieved fame by a speech for the prosecution. The judge said encouragingly that he thought I would do it quite well. I put my thoughts in order, which did not take long, and then waited for news.

About midday, Du Parcq came back and concluded his speech undramatically.

Then came the speech we had all been waiting for.

The case for the prosecution seemed unanswerable. The medical evidence established conclusively that Mrs Thomas had been poisoned by arsenic. The defence had made no attempt to refute it; they had called no evidence to challenge that of Dr Roche Lynch. Mrs Hearn had access to arsenic; the bottle of weedkiller was found in the gardener's shed. The first symptoms of arsenical poisoning appeared in Mrs Thomas within an hour or so after she had eaten the sandwich prepared by Mrs Hearn. If there was room for any suggestion that the arsenic had got into Mrs Thomas' body in some other way, the poisoning of the sister Minnie by arsenic and the fact that Mrs Hearn was nursing her for seven months before her death refuted it.

The judge then devoted a good deal of time to what seems to me in retrospect to be a negligible point. A witness can be cross-examined as to credit, that is, that she is not a person who can be believed on her oath. For that purpose instances of falsehoods otherwise irrelevant can be put to her in cross-examination. Mrs Hearn had described herself as a married woman. She said that she was married on 6 June 1919 to Mr Hearn, who left her shortly after: since then she had never seen nor heard of him. The marriage was in a registry office near Bedford Square. Her husband was Leonard Wilmot Hearn, a medical student; later she saw in a newspaper that he had died on 12 June.

It seems rather a pathetic case of a woman who did not wish to be known as a lifelong spinster and who wanted the title of Mrs. But what had it to do with murder by poisoning? It was introduced to show that she was not a woman who could be believed on her oath. The only evidence that she had given on oath and which was challenged was the stock answer to Mr Birkett's formal question, 'Have you ever administered arsenic to any person in any shape or form?' She said, 'No', and it is difficult to imagine anyone saying, 'Yes'.

Mr Birkett's speech was a masterpiece of attractive irrelevance. He had only two sound points to make. The first was that she had bought arsenic and kept it for four years without using it. The second point was that this was a motiveless murder. There was no evidence at all to support the suggestion that Mrs Hearn had hoped to become the second Mrs Thomas.

The summing up began on the next day. It was a massive presentation of the case for the prosecution: it could hardly be anything else.

Neither Birkett nor I were in court for it, Birkett because he had another case beginning in London and me because Du Parcq, who was fully recovered, was willing to release me, and the Attorney wanted me. We travelled to London in the same train, Birkett and his clerk travelling first class and myself third in conformity with our respective incomes. When the train got to Newton Abbott, Birkett came running down the platform waving a newspaper with the stop press news 'Not guilty'. I congratulated him upon his achievement. I do not now remember what I thought about it at the time; I did not know what lead the judge had given to the jury in his summing up though I strongly suspected that it would be towards a conviction.

Reading it now it strikes me as a masterly summary of the facts and issues. The facts are stated quite neutrally and there is no overt attempt to tell the jury what to do. There was no need for that; a clear statement of the hard evidence leads inevitably to a conclusion of guilt. He did however give a broad hint, but it was in two parts that would have to be put together. In an early part of his summing up he told the jury that the issue lay between Mrs Hearn and Mr Thomas. In a later part he dealt with the possibility of a 'conspiracy' between the two. A conspiracy in law need not mean plotters in black cloaks and masks moving stealthily; it means more than two or more people having a common understanding to bring about an agreed end; he reviewed the evidence and gave convincing reasons why there was no such understanding. But if one or the other of them had done it and they were not in it together, the finger, pointed away from Mr Thomas. He had not prepared the sandwiches: Mrs Hearn had. He had not been by Minnie's bedside for seven months: Mrs Hearn had.

But I doubt if the jury dwelt much on these sharper points. The summing up took four hours and twenty minutes to deliver. The jury considered their verdict for only fifty-two minutes. It took only that time to achieve unanimity contrary to the lead they had been given by the judge. They must have proceeded on broader lines than have yet been considered. Neither the judge nor the Crown devoted any time to the absence of motive: certainly the Crown has not got to prove motive. I did not, as I have said, give much thought to the verdict at the time. Juries were then thought to be more wayward than they are today and Welsh and Cornish juries were always suspected of eccentricities. Looking at it again, sixty years later, it seems to me that there were some odd things about the case.

First, motiveless poisonings are very rare; indeed I cannot think of one. Mrs Hearn's supposed ambition to be the second Mrs Thomas was no more than gossip which Mr Birkett rightly dismissed as fantastic. As for the sister Minnie, the only motive suggested was that an admittedly devoted sister had got tired of nursing her. A poisoner without a strong motive is a very rare specimen and I doubt if the trial gave sufficient attention to this. I can perhaps say this without inviting the accusation of being wise after the event. I am reported as concluding my opening speech to the magistrates with this paragraph:

> *It is no part of my duty to indulge in speculation as to the particular kind of motive which may or may not have promoted this woman to do what, in my*

submission, she has done. No man can judge the contents of another's heart. It would certainly be unsafe, in searching for motives, to search for motives such as would control the actions of ordinary men and women. If you assume that this woman did indeed commit this murder, if she could devise so terrible a means of killing, if she could inflict and watch the infliction of arsenic upon the bodies of two defenceless women – her sister and an innocent and kindly neighbour – she must obviously be the possessor of a mind so warped and so completely unmoved by the ordinary ideas which govern right thinking people, that the impression of things that to us might be trivial might be sufficiently great to have led her to commit this crime.[1]

Another thing is that the Crown did not appear to consider what sort of a woman Mrs Hearn was and what impression she might be making on the jury. I did not notice her during the twenty-one days of the committal proceedings (much of which was occupied by Mr West, her solicitor). At the makeshift court at Launceston, counsel were in the front row immediately beneath the dais, Mrs Hearn was directly behind with a wardress on either side of her. She was reported as being completely at ease and chatting happily to the wardresses; occasionally she would write a little note for Mr West. As I saw her at the court of trial she was always entirely composed. The judge noted the evidence which he said was much in her favour, that she was a devoted sister and an excellent nurse. The contents of her home had been inspected by the Crown and they were just what any chapel-going woman might be expected to have. There was an occasion during the long and painful illness when Minnie told the doctor that she thought she was being poisoned. Mrs Hearn said only 'Oh Minnie, how could you say such a thing.'

These were the days when the death penalty was automatic and when the jury was starkly confronted with the knowledge that, if they gave the word, this woman would within a few weeks be hanged. If she were guilty, Mr Birkett had said, she must be 'a human fiend'. This is no exaggeration and it may be that it is the question which the jury asked itself and answered no. They could not otherwise have reached that verdict so quickly – in fifty-two minutes after a summing up of four hours. For myself I think now that it was a Jekyll and Hyde case, a case of split personality, a case for a psychiatrist if by 1931 psychiatry had advanced that far.

A year or so later I met Mr West walking to the Temple along the Embankment. He told me that Mrs Hearn – under another name of course – had got a very good job as cook-housekeeper. It is said that a successful poisoner cannot resist the temptation of poisoning again. Mrs Hearn's case proved the rule, but only to a point. I have not since the trial come across any poisoning case that was remotely like hers, but I am no sort of criminologist.

[1] Evening Standard. 24th February 1931.

The Crown and the prosecution each devoted an appreciable amount of time to the 'Mrs' in Mrs Hearn. Certainly the circumstances of her marriage, as she recounted them, were very unusual. She had not a marriage certificate. She had never heard of 'marriage lines' and did not know what they were. It seems obvious that some twenty years before she had wished to be thought a married woman rather than a spinster. Both Mr Du Parcq and the judge pressed her about this and the judge referred to it in his summing up. The jury may have thought this to be hardly worth the dredging.

In 1886, fourteen years or thereabouts before Mrs Hearn was born, Robert Louis Stevenson wrote *Dr Jekyll and Mr Hyde*. It is an elaboration of the hypothesis that the human mind is made up of the good and the bad. Dr Jekyll was a good man and a prosperous doctor who experimented with this theory. He invented a potion which would make the bad side of him uppermost and another potion which would bring him back to normal again. In his second personality he calls himself Mr Hyde. The two personalities took different physical shapes, Dr Jekyll being a large and benevolent man and Mr Hyde a nasty and stunted one. As Mr Hyde he did villainous deeds, even committing murder, as his worst instincts prompted him. Today more is known about mind and body and the idea of a dual personality is not inconceivable.

Is it conceivable that while the lawyers were trying Hyde the person the jury saw was Jekyll? Surely they were not seeing the same personality as the judge. The jury did not have to decide between different personalities. Certainly there were two Mrs Hearns. There was the Mrs Hearn who devoted her life to nursing the sick and there was the Mrs Hearn who poisoned, in the most painful way, three women whom she was nursing. The jury cannot in the time that they took have seriously considered the summing up. They can only have asked themselves the question, on which they got no help from the prosecution or from the judge, was Mrs Hearn the sort of person who could have committed these murders? Was she the human fiend who could watch the day by day death of a sister dying in sickness and pain by her hand? If the answer to that was in doubt, then they had to acquit.

One way or another Norman Birkett must have got them to see the case in this light. That he did so was one of his greatest triumphs as an advocate for the defence.

Chapter XII

THE KYLSANT CASE

IN JULY I left Cornwall to go back to London and in that month the Kylsant case began in Court No. 1 at the Old Bailey. It was a complicated city fraud which an accountant, Sir William McLintock, had unearthed. To master its detail, the Attorney had a number of consultations with Sir William at which I was present and I was in court throughout. But it was not the sort of case in which I could be of much use.

Lord Kylsant was a Welsh businessman who had served his time in the House of Commons and had been rewarded with a peerage in 1918. Neither he nor Mr Morland his accountant, who stood beside him in the dock, looked at all like city tricksters. Lord Kylsant had been born a younger son of the 12th baronet of his line. He had been an MFH and a Lord Lieutenant. The accountant, Mr Morland, was a partner in the firm of Price Waterhouse, as well known then as it is today. What they were alleged to have done was to issue a balance sheet calculated to deceive the shareholders of the company about its true financial position and/or any members of the public who might be thinking of buying its shares.

The company concerned was the Royal Mail Steam Packet Company, the chairman being Lord Kylsant. The company owned and operated a fleet of cargo-carrying ships; it was one of the old companies that had been created by charter. Kylsant was an active chairman and did not challenge his responsibility for what the company did. Shipping was one of the industries that during the First World War made enormous profits, so large that an Excess Profits Tax was imposed. Prudently the Royal Mail added large sums to its reserves. 1920 was not only the last of the boom years; after it the company never had another year in which it made a trading profit. It lived on its wartime reserves. Those disclosed in the balance sheet for the year 1926 consisted of a Reserve Fund and an Insurance Fund together amounting to £1,700,000. In each year except 1926 the company declared a dividend of around 5% on the Ordinary Stock. The disclosed funds would have been insufficient to pay these dividends. In 1924, for example, the amount shown as transferred from the Reserve Fund was £150,000; in that year there was a trading loss of £900,000.

The bulk of the money that paid the dividends came from what were called hidden or secret reserves. Some of them consisted of non-recurring profits: none came from current trading. The secret reserves were not hidden in the sense that they were not known about by the top people in the management of the company's affairs. They were hidden from those shareholders who studied the balance sheets. A dividend is paid out of profits, and reserves are formed out of undistributed profits. If a steady diminution of reserves is shown in the balance sheet, shareholders might begin to ask questions and wonder about the company's future.

It was about this time, that is, at the end of the First World War, the victorious countries were disclosing that all of them except the United States were parties to secret treaties distributing the spoils of victory. It is generally agreed that diplomacy of this sort cannot be carried out in the open. In the first of the Fourteen Points in which President Wilson tabulated the objects for which the allies were fighting, he demanded 'open covenants, openly arrived at'. In the discussions in Paris which preceded the Treaty this was generally considered to be impracticable. All practising accountants seem to take the same view of hidden reserves, that is, that they are not wrong *per se*. But the two leading accountants called by the prosecution, Lord Plender and Sir William McLintock, agreed that the payment of dividends out of undisclosed reserves had in the Kylsant case gone on for so long - six consecutive years of heavy losses – as to give a false impression of the company's position. This was the nub of the prosecution's case.

It was not an easy case to put before a jury. Apart from the fact that it all had to be conducted in the language of balance sheets with which most of the jury would not be familiar (there was, as it happened, one of them who was a chartered accountant) the case did not raise the clear and simple commonsense point in which a jury is naturally in its element. Juries nowadays are told to acquit if they have any 'lurking doubt', a phrase that is now very popular with counsel for the defence. Doubts will always lurk in cases which the jury finds it difficult to understand.

The Act which made a false balance sheet an offence stipulated that it should be 'false in a material particular'. The phraseology suggests something clear and precise, something more precise than that the effect of a balance sheet was to misrepresent the true position of the company. But the construction of a statute is a question of law for the judge to decide and he ruled that it would make the balance sheet false in a material particular.

The case was one to bring out all the great talents of the Attorney-General. As a lawyer he convinced the judge of what is now the accepted construction of the statute. As an advocate he excelled in putting a complicated case in a way which the ordinary juryman could understand. He put it as a case in which a trading company had made a large trading loss for six consecutive years. At the time of the last balance sheet in 1927 it was, he said, a company which was on the rocks. Disaster inevitably lay ahead: the situation was one that could not truthfully be concealed from the shareholders.

There were two features which distinguished the case of the accountant, Mr Morland, so that in the end the Attorney General did not press for his conviction and he was acquitted.

The first of these was that in 1927 the company had issued a prospectus with which Mr Morland had nothing to do. It offered debenture stock of £2,000,000 to the public. It said nothing material about the company's position, except that it was making profits sufficient to pay the interest on the new debentures five times over. To say that the interest was being paid from current trading and not from running down assets was surely false.

The second thing was that in Lord Kylsant's case there was a motive for wrongdoing. But Mr Morland got nothing from the fraud, except an auditor's fee of 400 guineas. The terms of Kylsant's contract gave him a personal motive for keeping the company alive. As Chairman he was paid a salary of £3,000 per annum plus a commission of $1/2\%$ of the company's assumed profit (i.e. the amount paid on dividends on the ordinary stock) provided that the dividend declared was not less than 5%. There had been only one year for which it had not been fulfilled and that was in 1926 when the dividend declared was 4%. Usually in the 1920s he earned between £20,000 and £30,000 per year.

There was a great array of leading counsel. The Attorney General had with him D. N. Pritt K.C.. Sir John Simon K.C. for Lord Kylsant had with him Mr Singleton K.C.. Sir Patrick Hastings for Mr Morland had not only Mr Stuart Bevan K.C., but also Mr C. J. Conway K.C.. Mr Justice Wright, an experienced commercial judge, tried the case. Today cases of serious fraud are expected to last for months. The trial of this case was set down to begin on 20 July allowing only nine working days before the end of term. The trial was concluded on 30 July, the summing up took four hours and the jury took three hours to consider their verdict. They found Lord Kylsant guilty and he was sentenced to one year's imprisonment.

It is unthinkable today that a case as complicated as the Kylsant case would be put down for trial with only ten working days before the long vacation. It could have been made to look as difficult as any serious fraud case and it could have been made to last as long. But in 1931 a fortnight was a long time for any case to take. In this instance the defendants were represented by highly skilled counsel. They were all men of the top quality who had learned by practice how to say a great deal in a short time.

Chapter XIII

THE FALL OF THE GOVERNMENT

THE LONG vacation began on the 1st August and I had already made my plans. I had made friends with a girl[1] whose mother liked to spend summer abroad. The mother had a large and comfortable Packard car, chauffeur driven, and she invited her daughter to take a friend with her. Whether the sex of the friend had been mentioned was not quite clear.

Early in August we crossed via Harwich to the Hook of Holland, and motored in a leisurely way up the Rhine. Apart from the trip to Paris I had never been to Europe before. It was all very exciting. We spent a night or two in Cologne and Nuremberg, and a little longer in Heidelberg; some days in Munich; then at a small lakeside hotel in Austria, some days in Cadenabbia in the Italian lakes and in Verona and then turned back to go by Zurich into France.

It was somewhere in France and towards the end of August that we picked up rumours of a Government crisis in Britain. The origin of the crisis is now traced back to the decision of the Conservative government in 1925, when Winston Churchill was Chancellor of the Exchequer, to make gold once again the anchor of the currency.

Before the war which broke out at 11.00 pm on 4 August 1914, the British currency consisted of coins minted by the Royal Mint from gold, silver and copper. Although banknotes for sums of £5 and upwards were widely in use, they were not legal currency. A £5 note was only a promissory note by a bank to pay £5 to the person presenting it. Legal tender, if the creditor insisted on it, was the coinage of the realm stamped by the Mint with the King's head. Coinage issued by the Mint was of a prescribed weight and fineness of gold, silver or copper. The most valuable unit which was minted as currency was the gold sovereign. Until 5 August 1914 gold in this form circulated as freely as silver and copper. Every gentleman had his sovereign case with a series of little compartments into which the sovereign and the half sovereign neatly fitted and from which it could be extricated by finger and thumb without being jostled by copper and silver. It was out of such a case as I have said that a benevolent uncle used to give each of us nephews and nieces a half sovereign every Christmas.

At the beginning of the 1914-18 war all gold coinage had to be handed over to the government in exchange for a Treasury note of a denomination of £1 for the

[1] Madeleine Oppenheimer whom he married in 1932.

138

sovereign and ten shillings for the half sovereign. This proved to be the end of gold as currency but not the end of the 'gold standard'. The gold standard prescribed the weight and fineness of the gold which was minted into sovereigns. It could be, and had in the past been, debased by clipping. In modern times it would be debased by an instruction to the Mint to lower the amount or fineness of gold that the sovereign was to contain; this is devaluation by lowering the standard. Presumably at some time during the war as inflation increased we did devalue: what the act of 1925 did was to restore 'parity' with gold. It was acclaimed by all parties in Britain as reincarnating the city of London as the financial market of the world.

We were all very pleased with ourselves in 1925 when the country went back to gold. After it happened I went to a speech by Lloyd George (one of the few statesmen who made a personal contribution to winning the War) in which he rejoiced oratorically in the event. He lowered his right hand almost to the floor and then raised it up on high saying, 'The pound can now look the dollar in the face'. It was this rather than the practical realities that made the crisis of 1931. Devaluation would mean that we were back on the floor again. The uncontrolled devaluation of the mark after the defeat of Germany to a point where its price was below the price of producing the paper it was written on was feared as if it was the plague.

The return to gold in 1925 did not bring back the sovereign. The nation still needed to conserve its supplies of the precious metal. What we returned to was the 'standard'. This would have been all right if gold of the specified weight and fineness always fetched the same price, that is, if gold was as Shakespeare puts it, 'as constant as the northern star of whose true-fixed and resting quality there is no fellow in the firmament'. But the price of gold fluctuated like everything else according to the law of supply and demand, though no doubt it fluctuated more sedately than most. Today there are more subtle ways of managing the currency than that of tying it to a marketable metal but in 1930 devices such as the Exchange Rate Mechanism were yet to be discovered. Traders who priced themselves out of the market have to cut their prices to retain their trade. Trading nations cut their prices by devaluation. But in 1931 this was heresy which the Bank of England and the Treasury could not contemplate.

Serious inflation began with the war of 1914. As children we noted it by the rise in the price of the 'bulls-eye', a peppermint sweet with black and white stripes: at the beginning of the War, bulls-eyes were 20 for a penny, by the end of it they were 8 or 10.

The 1930s are remembered as a decade of depression ending in another great war. The Labour government was unlucky in coming into office in 1929. The electorate had returned it to power as the largest party but the majority was not large enough to defeat both the Conservatives and the Liberals when they combined. However the Conservatives under Mr Baldwin took the view that the country, by giving the Labour party the largest vote, thought that it ought to be given a chance to see what it could do; and the Liberals were generally co-operative.

The economic position of the country, and indeed of much of the world, went from bad to worse in the thirties. Unemployment increased by leaps and bounds. The demands on the unemployment fund went up and up. Mr Snowden, the Chancellor of the Exchequer, was an orthodox financier. The individual who falls on bad times has to cut his coat according to his cloth. Snowden thought that the nation should act likewise; he would have nothing to do with expansionist economics which Maynard Keynes was beginning to make fashionable. The idea that a nation should spend its way out of a depression instead of retrenching was anathema to him. The budget must be balanced. Trade being bad, the number of the unemployed was steadily increasing, the unemployment fund was always in deficit and always borrowing. In February 1931 the Conservatives put down a motion censuring the government for the continuous additions to public expenditure. The Liberals softened the attack with an amendment demanding an independent committee to advise the Chancellor on all possible legitimate reductions consistent with efficiency.

The Cabinet decided that it would accept the Liberal amendment. The debate began on 11 February. The Chancellor warned the House about the disasters that would follow any suspicion that Britain's budgetary position was unsound, and called on the nation 'to put its financial house in order'. (Was this the birth of the 'house in order' cliché?) The Liberal amendment was carried by 468 votes to 21; this ought to have been taken as a warning: the 21 dissidents consisted of Labour but a larger group of Labour members abstained. The independent committee's report proved to be the catalyst which transformed the financial crisis into a political crisis. It was called the May Report after the name of its chairman and was delivered on the worst day of the year, 30 July, when everyone who mattered was going away on holiday. On 23 July the bank rate had been raised in anticipation to 3.5%; the day the report was delivered it was raised again to 4.5%. The report forecast a huge budget deficit of £120m and recommended cuts in expenditure totalling £97m of which £67m was in expenditure on the unemployed.

On the next day, 31 July, the Prime Minister left for Lossiemouth, his birthplace, in the North of Scotland to begin his summer holiday. It was also the beginning of his decline. He had raised himself from nothing to the leadership of a new party with a new outlook. I would hazard a guess that he is still the greatest figure the Labour party has produced. If he was vain, he had much to be vain about, notably his achievements in foreign affairs, his handling of his cabinets and in his prime his powers of oratory. He was ready to put his country before his party: that the disaster which he failed to avert was only imaginary does not diminish the virtue.

He began by writing to Keynes asking for his views on the May Report. Keynes replied immediately that his views on the subject were not fit for publication. The May Report was, he said, an attempt to make the existing deflation effective and would result in a gross perversion of social justice and a substantial increase in unemployment. Anyway, he wrote, it is now nearly certain that we shall go off the existing gold parity: we can put this off for a time, he said, by borrowing francs and dollars but this is the equivalent of admitting that 'the game is up'. He suggested a devaluation of not less than 25%. The 'existing deflation' to which Keynes referred was the rise in the value of the pound consequent upon the return to the Gold Standard in 1925.

Other economists consulted were more cautious; Hubert Henderson wrote that the time had not yet been reached for devaluation and advised on a substantial proportion of the savings recommended by the May committee. MacDonald rejected the Keynes solution. 'It was' his biographer writes 'the most tragic, as well as the most disastrous, mistake of MacDonald's life'.[1]

The matter was then referred to a Cabinet sub-committee which reported to the Cabinet on 19 August. Immediately on receipt of the report the Cabinet sat from 11.00 am until 10.30 pm with intervals for refreshment. That evening at 9.30 pm they met a deputation from the TUC led by Walter Citrine as the General Secretary, and Ernest Bevin. The TUC, Citrine said, would not acquiesce in new burdens on the unemployed: he was followed by Bevin who added that the TUC would not support a continuation of the deflation policy.

On the following day, 20 August, MacDonald and Snowden met Neville Chamberlain, who was speaking for the Conservatives, while Mr Baldwin was still on holiday at Aix-les-Bains. It was not a success. The opposition demanded more drastic action on unemployment insurance, including a cut in benefit.

The choice appeared to be between abandoning parity or cutting unemployment benefit. A cabinet meeting on 21 August at 10.00 am decided to reject the TUC's representation. The question that mattered was how to increase the savings on unemployment insurance. Someone took the point that a cut of 11.5% would correspond with the fall in the cost of living since the government had taken office: it would yield £15m. There was no support for this. On 10% to yield £12.5m the cabinet was equally divided. No attempt seems to have been made to justify the 10% by pointing out that rather more than that represented the fall in the cost of living. Nevertheless MacDonald put 10% to the opposition leaders, Chamberlain

[1] *Ramsay MacDonald*. David Marquand. Jonathan Cape. 1977. p. 614.

with Sir Herbert Samuel for the Liberals, and was told that it was wholly unsatisfactory and would lead to defeat as soon as Parliament reassembled. The opposition suggested that the King should be informed. They said that if MacDonald wished to form a government with their co-operation they were willing to serve under him.

It was now clear that the only solution which anyone could see was the cut in unemployment benefit. It seems at first sight to be surprising that no one argued that a cut of 10% was not really a cut at all but a return to the level in cost of living terms of 1929. Personally I would have accepted the logic of that but not the conclusion to where the logic led.

One of the minor benefits arising from my services to the Attorney General was that I had been appointed a counsel to the Ministry of Labour. My task was to prosecute in one or other of the London Magistrates Courts unemployed persons who were charged with obtaining benefit under false pretences. The magistrates had a difficult task. The accused were invariably guilty. The benefit in those days was called 'the dole' and this was what it was, a sum just large enough to keep the beneficiary and his family from starvation but not enough to fortify against temptation. If you are living on the margin above starvation and your income is suddenly decreased by 10%, you will not know how to make ends meet; it will be no consolation to you to be told that over the past five years your income had been invisibly increasing.

But the law was the law, and magistrates had to enforce it. Most magistrates did their best and either imposed a small fine with a long time to pay or even a short prison sentence. But there were a few who delivered sanctimonious addresses on the wickedness of biting the hand that fed and who imposed substantial sentences. On the other hand, there was one man who had been a Liberal member of Parliament and who appeased his conscience by taking ridiculous points of law for the defence and finding the accused not guilty. It was a pitiful business and I could well understand an obstinate opposition to any cuts at all.

For the Labour government there was a three-fold choice. They could do the cuts themselves; they could resign and let the opposition do them or they could pursue the still nebulous idea of a national government. Devaluation as recommended by Keynes was not even mentioned.

23 August was the crucial day. The Bank of England was getting down to its last gold bar. To go off gold, was then considered to be a fate worse than death and/or dishonour by all apart from Keynes and perhaps a few other economists. It was hardly more than ten years since the world had seen the German mark being bought and sold at a figure less than the value of the paper it was printed on. The situation could not await the recall of Parliament: a solution of some sort must be

found at once. On 22 August, the day before, the Bank of England had asked the Americans for a temporary loan and they were still awaiting the answer. At 7.00 pm the Cabinet met and waited to hear it; it came from the Federal Reserve Bank about 9.00 pm. The most that the Bank would offer was a short-term credit of $150m, conditional on the French offering a similar amount. The Bank assumed that the governments's programme would have the support of the Bank of England and the city generally. The Prime Minister made a great effort to persuade the Cabinet to accept and the vote was 11 in favour and 9 against but it was clear that some at least of the 9 would resign. The Prime Minister had told the Cabinet that if there were any important resignations, the government must resign as a whole. He now told the Cabinet that he would advise the King to confer the following morning with Baldwin, Samuel and himself.

The King told MacDonald that he was the only man who could lead the country through the crisis and asked him to reconsider his decision. By 10.35 am the next morning it had been agreed that Baldwin and Samuel would serve under MacDonald in a national government to last until an emergency bill had been passed by Parliament; after that the King would grant a dissolution. The national government would be not a 'coalition' but a 'co-operation'; each party would in the election fight by itself for its own programme.

In the new cabinet of eight ministers, National Labour, as it came to call itself, had four places including the Prime Minister and the Conservatives also had four; the Liberals had two. This was done on 25 August.

The formation of the national government did not bring the hoped for solution. The withdrawals of gold and foreign exchange continued. On 15 September the Invergordon 'mutiny' was a protest against pay cuts. There was another run on the Bank which cost the reserves more than £30m. Applications for further foreign credits were turned down and 'silently and solemnly'[1], as MacDonald put it, the government agreed to go off gold. The silence and solemnity must have been due to the fact that it was hardly more than a month since the national government had been formed to avert this catastrophe.

The subsequent devaluation came very near to Keynes's estimate of 25%. On 21 September the Gold Standard (Amendment) Bill was passed through all its stages. On 7 October Parliament was dissolved and the ensuing general election was on 27 October. The Labour party paid the penalty of having found the right solution a little too early. Defeat is too weak a word to describe what happened to the party in that election. It was not merely defeated but almost annihilated for its failure to save the pound. The Labour party was reduced to 52 members of whom 6 were members of the Independent Labour Party. Only one member of the old Labour

[1] ibid p. 659.

cabinet, George Lansbury, kept his seat. The Conservatives had 471 members and with their supporters, Simonite Liberals and the National Labour group they had a majority of 556. In the country the government parties polled 14.5 million votes to Labour's 6.5 million. Nothing like it has been seen before or since.

At an early stage, before the breach with the old Labour party became irreparable, MacDonald had written to all the ministers who were not in the Cabinet inviting them to resume their posts. Only one or two of them accepted. They included Jowitt who remained Attorney General. They did not include Stafford Cripps who from the first played a larger role in party affairs than Jowitt did. He wrote a polite refusal saying that he could not agree with the Prime Minister's new policy.

Jowitt's position was a difficult one. Joining with the National Labour party meant that he had to leave his new party less than three years after he had joined it. He sat as one of the two members for Preston. His constituency party of course refused to adopt him and he didn't feel that he could offer himself as a candidate in opposition to those who had adopted him before. Had he foreseen the devastating victory achieved by government supporters and the size of the personal victory of the Prime Minister in his old Labour seat, he might have acted differently. For Ramsay MacDonald stood in his old constituency. In 1929 as the Labour candidate he had been returned with a majority of 28,000. He had represented the constituency for less than three years during which time he cannot as Prime Minister have had any time to cultivate it. The Labour party candidate, Coxon, whom he now opposed, was a local man who had been his agent in the 1929 election. All the press expected MacDonald to be defeated and then to seek a safe Conservative seat. In the result he was elected with a majority of nearly 6,000 over Coxon.

All that offered itself to Jowitt was a place among the candidates who competed for a university seat. While Oxford and Cambridge had two members each, the remaining 'combined universities', as they were called, had only one, in which the sitting member, an independent, was a highly respected woman candidate. There was no campaigning - each candidate circulated his or her address. Jowitt had no ties with any provincial university. He was seeking election as a refugee and as such it cannot have assisted him that he had supported a Labour motion putting an end to university representation. He was defeated.

Notwithstanding this defeat, he was in the new government as Attorney-General. A law officer was so much needed in the House then he could not do his work properly without a seat in the Commons. The leaders of the Conservative and Liberal parties seem to have made a genuine effort to provide him with a seat, but seats are in the hands of the local party – and no one was anxious to surrender his seat to a Labour refugee. The government of course had an enormous majority and the opposition was fragmented.

There were thereafter two or three possibilities – one, I think, was at Montrose - but none of them came to anything. In January Jowitt gave up the search and Lesley and he went off for a winter holiday in Portugal (Estoril, north of Lisbon, was just becoming fashionable as a winter resort) before resuming his practice at the Bar.

So, in February 1932, I was out of a job. Nonetheless I had considerably improved my position. Instead of being penniless and briefless, I had the Mint and the Ministry of Labour and in theory, at any rate, I was in a better position to pick up what small briefs were going and indeed I did pick up one very quickly, but I would have to make an entirely new start.

Chapter XIV

THE CHRISTIE-MILLER CASE

ONE DAY, in March 1932, while I was still in the cubby hole, I was informed by Adams, the head clerk in person, that a partner in Bischoff Cox had asked for a conference in a case which he named as Christie-Miller and to which he would be bringing a young man in the office who was reading for his articles.

Mr Bischoff had a strange story to unfold. Mrs Christie- Miller, a lady in opulent circumstances, lived at Clarendon Park near Salisbury. While she was away from home a criminal, who was easily caught and identified, broke into her house and got away with several articles of dress and not much else. Since he pleaded guilty and the case was obviously a simple one it was thought safe to commit the prisoner for trial at the Devizes Quarter Sessions where Mr Robert Seton the Associate was the Recorder with an annual stipend of £50. At the committal proceedings Mrs Christie-Miller made her deposition identifying the articles stolen and was bound over in her own recognizances in the sum of £10 to give evidence at the sessions.

She found this to be inconvenient since she would be abroad. She consulted her friend, the Chief Constable of Wiltshire, who promised to arrange matters so that her trip abroad would not be interfered with. He ascertained that the Recorder was at Winchester Assizes discharging his duty as Associate. So he spoke to the Chief Constable of Hampshire who undertook to send a young constable to see Mr Seton at Winchester and to ask whether Mrs Christie-Miller, whose part in the drama was so small, could be excused from attendance, 'Of course,' said Robert, 'Mrs Christie-Miller of Clarendon Park, I know her well.'

A couple of months or more passed before the date for the Devizes Sessions. Robert was distressed to find that the police in accordance with their usual practice had allowed only this one simple case to go to Devizes and felt that he had to make the most of it.

His memory was erratic and I am sure that he had genuinely forgotten his conversation about Mrs Christie-Miller when he repelled the prosecuting counsel's suggestion that he could decide upon an appropriate sentence from the facts recorded in the depositions. Mrs Christie-Miller, he said, was a very important witness and it was necessary that the articles stolen should be more precisely identified: 'Let her name be called.' It was called and unsurprisingly there was no answer. This, said Robert, was disgraceful and a serious interference with the course of justice. Why had she not appeared? It so happened that the young constable who had spoken to the Recorder in Winchester was at the Devizes court where the Chief Constable of Hampshire with some foreshadowing of Robert's eccentricities had told him to be. He stood up and began to explain. Robert, with perhaps some hazy perception that things were not going according to plan, said, 'Shut up.' All this was recorded almost verbatim in the local newspapers, the *Wiltshire News* and the *Wiltshire Gazette*. Robert concluded the proceedings by saying that Mrs Christie-Miller, who was treating his court with 'extreme impertinence and contempt', must attend at his next sessions to show cause why she should not forfeit her recognizances.

Continuing with his narrative, Mr Bischoff said that Mrs Christie-Miller would certainly appear at the next Quarter Sessions. She was anxious to do so (and as a less decorous solicitor might have added, to give the Recorder a piece of her mind) and he would instruct me to represent her. Was there, in the meanwhile, any other step that she should take?

Although I had had no idea about what the subject of the conference would be, I did know something about the Christie-Miller case. In fact it had been a matter for speculation throughout the circuit. What was Robert going to do? Although naturally a talkative man, always willing to gossip and far from the soul of discretion, Robert had resisted all attempts to extract even an inkling of his intentions.

I suggested that if Mrs Christie-Miller was anxious to do something, money being no object, she could move in the High Court for a writ of prohibition forbidding Robert to hear and determine the issue of whether recognizances should be forfeited on the ground that it was not one that he could decide impartially. I said that there was really no answer to this but that I thought that the Chief Justice, Lord Hewart, would probably find some way round it and that Mrs Christie-Miller's money would be wasted. Mr Bischoff said that Mrs Christie-Miller would probably adhere to her view that money was no object in a good cause and that he would take instructions.

In due course I was instructed to move for a writ of prohibition. Affidavits were prepared and obtained from all the witnesses in the chain of evidence along which the rashly spoken words of the Recorder had been conveyed to Mrs Christie-Miller. These were zealously prepared by David Pollock, Mr Bischoff's articled clerk. It was he who, having some hazy recollection that I was a person who had spoken at the Cambridge Union, though we had never met before, had picked my name out of the list of counsel at the Devizes Sessions as one who might be expected to accept a brief at a moderate fee.

So the application for the writ was listed in a specially constituted divisional court consisting of the Lord Chief Justice and Mr Justice Talbot. I do not know about

Talbot J. but Lord Hewart followed his usual practice of making up his mind first and listening afterwards. He remained silent throughout except for one intervention. He inquired whether it was not my proper course to allow the matter to proceed and to apply to the court after the matter had been clarified by the Recorder. I said that that would still leave an issue as to who was to pay the costs. 'Costs against whom?' Lord Hewart asked in a withering tone. But I had researched that one and replied correctly, 'Costs out of the County Fund.'

So the witnesses to Robert's complicity were subpoenaed for the next sessions, including the two Chief Constables who, though busy men, cheerfully agreed. Accompanied by David Pollock, I went down to Devizes on the appointed day.

I had made an initial blunder which might have been fatal. It was unwise to rate Robert as an old bumbler: he was in truth a very wily man. These events occurred before the Act of 1933 which abolished Grand Juries. As I explained on page 85, before that time the first step in the proceedings at Sessions or Assizes was for the judge to address the Grand Jury and to sit in court waiting for the true bills to be conveyed in an antique manner to the court of trial. During these proceedings – this was what I had forgotten – it was the strict rule that no counsel should be in court. So I remained in the robing room with other counsel waiting for the announcement that the business of the sessions was about to begin. I had supposed that one of these pieces of business would be the affair Christie-Miller. But what Robert now claimed to have done was not to have adjourned the Christie-Miller case to the next sessions, but to have adjourned the sessions themselves until the day mentioned.

I have an eye-witness account from David Pollock of what took place. Robert opened the door of his retiring room and peered round the court to make sure that his ruse had succeeded and that no counsel was in court. He then took his seat and saying that he would deal first with the business from the adjourned sessions before charging the Grand Jury and adding that he understood that Mrs Christie-Miller was in court ready to apologise for her absence on the last occasion, ordered that she should enter the witness box. Most fortunately David Pollock, to whom as a solicitor the ban did not apply, was in court. He rushed into the robing room and told me what was happening. I rushed into court and found that Mrs Christie-Miller was hovering uncertainly outside the witness box which she had been told to enter.

This was the last opportunity Robert had to behave sensibly. But his Recordership was his most prized possession and he felt, I suppose, somehow or other he had to preserve it. He would not of course estreat[1] her recognizances;

---

[1] Legal term meaning making a person surrender the money he or she pledged to guarantee his or her presence in court.

probably he had never intended to. But he was unwilling – few judges are – to pay the simple price of an apology. What he had hoped to do was to treat her appearance as an expression of contrition, which he would graciously accept. Of course, no barrister would let him get away with that; he staked a lot on his ruse of getting the case over before counsel knew anything about it.

But he had another string to his bow. He asked if I was going to dispute that he was a corporation sole. Corporations are in law of two kinds. There is the kind that everybody knows about, the limited liability companies which are formed by a number of shareholders and which the law endows with a legal personality of their own. The law gives also the same status to single persons who are the holders of certain public offices, I assume that he intended to argue that his, private and informal utterance did not bind the Recorder of Devizes as a corporation sole. But he did not pursue the point perhaps because his knowledge of corporations, whether sole or multiple was strictly limited. The point not being of 'human interest' was not one that attracted the reporters of the *News* and *Gazette* which are now my chief sources and I do not remember the detail of the argument. Like most of the points in the case it had an *Alice in Wonderland* character and dissolved itself without any conclusion.

I thought that the first thing to do was to get Mrs Christie-Miller out of the witness box. I said that I represented her and I submitted that the proper procedure as laid down by *Archbold* and the Court of Criminal Appeal was that, before recognizances could be estreated they must be proved to have been broken. When this had been done, I said, I should call evidence to show why she did not appear.

'Please do not interrupt' the Recorder said, 'I accept her appearance as satisfying me that there was no deliberate intention to defy the order of the court. No further punishment is necessary.' I asked if he would listen to the evidence.

The Recorder:	'I am afraid I must conduct this case in my own way. I only want to ask Mrs Christie-Miller a few questions. The point is here what answers she has. Of course it may be that there is medical evidence. I am not going to allow anything irrelevant.'
Me:	'When a case is made out I shall call evidence.'
The Recorder:	'The evidence must be relevant to Mrs Christie-Miller being ill or something of that sort. I am not going to allow you to call general hearsay.'
Me:	'I shall call no hearsay evidence, Sir.'

The Recorder then proceeded to deliver on his judgment:
'She has what is called purged her contempt. What took place at the Quarter

Sessions has nothing to do with this. I shall not allow that to be gone into. A very full and complete explanation has been given to me by the Chief Constable; I accept it unreservedly. It was due no doubt to a misunderstanding on the part of the Chief Constable and also on the part of some of the people under him. That explanation has been given to me and this is accepted. I shall not, therefore, allow anything further with regard to that. The police are always looked upon by the court as assisting them. I shall not allow any suggestions or attacks to be made with regard to their conduct. That excludes all that. Mrs Christie-Miller has appeared here and practically surrendered herself to the jurisdiction of the court as she must do. The case is over. It is only now a question of dealing with her and her alone.'

Me:	'With respect, Sir, I have not finished yet.'
The Recorder:	'What do you want to say further?'
Me:	'I want to call evidence which will be contrary to your view of the facts.'

The Recorder said it was not necessary to call evidence. Mrs Christie-Miller had surrendered and purged her contempt.
'I am of the opinion that quite sufficient punishment has been placed upon her and I accept her coming here as an acknowledgement that she feels she did not do what was right. I do not say whether she was badly advised or not. I am not going into that. She has properly accepted the order of the court and come. It is a sufficient for her to come here, therefore I do not order her recognizances to be estreated and she may now depart. The costs of this application cannot be allowed as costs against the county.'

Me:	'Will you listen to a submission? My submission is that Mrs Christie-Miller did not attend the last Session because she had permission from the very best authority, namely yourself. The explanation of the Chief Constable, such as you said you unreservedly accept, was before you a month or so ago. My client has been brought here and put to the expense of being represented before you and to the expense of bringing witnesses. She was bound to justify the truth of her story; she has been brought here unnecessarily. I apply for her cost to be reimbursed to that extent.'
The Recorder:	'Have you finished?'
Me:	'That is all I have to say on that point.'

The Recorder:	'What other point do you want to make?'

I said that I wanted an apology. The Recorder had said that Mrs Christie-Miller was treating the court with extreme impertinence and disrespect.

The Recorder denied that he had ever said anything like that; one could not, he said, rely on press reports. I said that I proposed to call the police officer to testify that he had heard the Recorder use those words; the Recorder said that he would not allow the police to be attacked. I said that he had apparently interviewed privately the Chief Constable with the knowledge that these proceedings were pending, as a result of which he had come to the conclusion that there must have been some misunderstanding; it was not a misunderstanding to which Mrs Christie-Miller had contributed in any way. The concluding words were on my part, that it was a 'monstrous injustice' that she should not be reimbursed the costs she had incurred. She should have received not punishment but an apology.

The Recorder:	'I have listened to the very able observations Mr Devlin has made with his usual ability and excellence, but I cannot accept all of them. The order of the court is "No costs".'

When the case was over, I wrote him a note saying that I was sorry that what I felt to be my duty to my client, had caused me to be rude to him. I got a letter back which I found entirely illegible accept for the ending, which was 'Your loving father Robert Seton'. I presumed that he had put a letter to one of his sons, to whom he was devoted, into the wrong envelope, but I did not investigate further. I frequently sat next to him as before and listened to his accounts of his time at Eton with Lord Curzon. Robert was a nice old thing, typical of the bumblers for whom 'somebody had done something'. It was somebody doing something for him which gave him the small Recordership which he cherished.

He was an old man and it was quite understandable that he should have forgotten that he had himself excused Mrs Christie-Miller's attendance. When he remembered it – and the proceedings in the High Court must have jogged his memory – he could have written her a letter of apology and regret and nothing more would have been heard of the matter; the writ of prohibition had not been granted, so that he could have escaped from the situation without indignity.

The Bar has had a long history of placemen who survive, some of them only on a pittance. Robert Seton was perhaps one of the last. His sons repaid his devotion quite a long time afterwards when Robert died; they were concerned that he should have a grand obituary in *The Times*. One of the sons wrote to Rayner Goddard, who was then Chief Justice and had been a member of the Western Circuit, to ask if he would write an obituary for *The Times*. Rayner declined as gracefully as possible. But some days later there appeared in *The Times* a very full obituary, complete with photograph. For the last time, 'somebody had done something' for Robert.

Cases such as Robert Seton's were beginning to die out in the first part of the twentieth century and I doubt if anything like them could be found today. They derived from a strong eighteenth century principle that no progress could be made in any profession without INFLUENCE. Jane Austen's beloved brother William, whom she puts into *Mansfield Park* as the younger brother of the heroine, could not expect to get on in the Navy without the influence of Admiral Crawford. Promotion depended upon the influential word. There is a story about Lord Ellenborough when he was Chief Justice. He was riding down the Strand from the Temple to Westminster Hall when he was given the message that his nominee for a reversion had suddenly died. He did not lose a minute: he turned his horse and rode back to the Temple and immediately made another nomination.

Up to the middle of the twentieth century, the idea that promotion should come entirely by merit was still quite feeble. A brief career in Parliament during which political strings could be pulled was still considered as one of the quickest ways of getting onto the Bench. The Whips of the party in power had ways of communicating with the Lord Chancellor. There is a story about Lord Halsbury, a die-hard Lord Chancellor. A cautious don, making conversation in the combination room said, 'I suppose, Lord Chancellor, that *ceteris paribus* you would appoint a Conservative rather than a Liberal to the High Court Bench.' Observing a frown on the Lord Chancellor's face, he hastily repeated '*ceteris paribus* of course, I mean.' But all Lord Halsbury said was, 'Damn *ceteris paribus*.' In 1927 most people to whom I talked about going to the Bar, would ask as their first question what INFLUENCE I had.

Captious critics may point out that it was the way in which both Colin Pearson and myself got on; we can plead only that since eventually we both ended up at the top of the ladder by more conventional steps, no harm can have been done.

Chapter XV

NO. 1 BRICK COURT – LEADS ON TO FORTUNE

ADAMS the head clerk, was evidently rather impressed by my solicitor client especially since Mr Bischoff followed that brief with another to advise jointly with Mr Wilfrid Greene K.C. on some point in the tangled affairs of the Gulbenkian family. Wilfrid Greene was then the most eminent counsel at the Chancery Bar, so eminent that he would not advise without a junior (who had to be paid two thirds of his leader's fee) to whom he would dictate his opinion. He was a charming man and it was all done in the most delightful way in consultation. Mr Bischoff and I went to his chambers. Mr Greene expounded his views pausing at various points to ask whether I agreed, which of course I did, and then he said 'let me sum up' and dictated fluently and easily what his opinion was. Mr Bischoff said he would like to have a written opinion so Mr Greene said, 'Then we shall ask Mr Devlin to write it.' Fortunately I had a good memory for that sort of thing and was able to reproduce it on paper almost verbatim. Then we both signed it and collected our handsome fees in due course.

This sort of thing was all very well but it occupied very little of my time. For the rest of it I was left to kick my heels. Field's two devils did all the work for him that was necessary; nobody else in chambers needed anything done for him at all. I would have liked to have gone back to devilling for William Jowitt but it was a firm doctrine at the Bar that to devil for a silk never got anybody anywhere. A junior's devil might expect, when the junior took silk, to step into his shoes as well as to take the junior briefs that his master was too busy to do. From the silk nothing of this sort could be expected .

A silk, when he becomes a law officer, moves into his room in the law courts taking his clerk with him. When he ceases to be a law officer he goes back to his chambers with his clerk. Jowitt's clerk, Edward Cheeseman, was not of the highest type. He had not the air of Adams; he had not any air at all. He was a little man, as I remember him, with a round face and spectacles and a chirpy manner when he was sober. A clerk naturally keeps his best surface for the head of his chambers who is his principal paymaster but he is wise in his own interests to have a care for a second, a third and even a fourth string.

Cheeseman seems to have neglected them and even antagonised them. Some of them were very distinguished. Donald Somerville was Attorney-General for a number of years and afterwards a law lord. Cys Asquith told me that when he joined chambers he was asked by Cheeseman for the customary guarantee of a minimum in clerk's fees but it was a good deal higher than Cys had expected. Cheeseman assured him that he was in a position to put a great deal of work in his way. When, after one or two barren years, Cys reminded him of this he produced a brief from a solicitor called Iohnson; at least that was what Cys thought he was called but it turned out that his real name was Johnson, Cheeseman's misfortune being that he had only one typewriter in the office and it had lost its Capital J.

But William Jowitt was devoted to him. He had, I suppose, been William's clerk from the beginning and, so far as a clerk can do it, had built up his practice. It is not unusual for a barrister who has made his way at the Bar to feel that much of his success was due to his clerk. In William's case it was difficult to believe that in fact it was. But William did so. So chambers said that they would be very pleased to have William back but that they would not stand for Cheeseman.

Possibly this did not disturb William very deeply. Why should he go back to cramped quarters in his old chambers when he was in a position to take any accommodation he wanted? There was vacant a set in the Temple which the Inn would make available for him. Their only disadvantage was that they were on the second floor. But even the most eminent solicitors were used to climbing two or more flights of stairs. What the eminent solicitors disliked, I think, was having to settle large fees for important clients with Cheeseman who was a crafty bargainer. But it was a firm rule in the Temple that a barrister never discussed his fees and lay clients, who would naturally expect a large fee to be agreed by a senior partner, just had to put up with it.

No. 1 Brick Court was a set of four rooms on the second floor. The principal rooms had a pleasing prospect to the south of the Middle Temple hall, the Temple gardens and the river. The smaller room on that side was the waiting room. The office accommodation looked north over Brick Court. One room was the clerk's room, and in the other William installed a secretary who could do typing and shorthand, at that time I believe the only such person in any set of chambers in London. The waiting room was also unique, a bit of swank that was hardly necessary since the lobby which gave access to all the rooms was more than adequate for the purpose.

William said that if I wanted to come into his chambers I could have the room that was kept as the clients' waiting room but he advised me strongly against it.

I cannot remember just how long after I had resumed my practice such as it was, I spent in Field's chambers. I do not think it was very long before I decided to reject the accepted wisdom and to chance my arm at No. 1 Brick Court.

I cannot remember quite when I took the plunge. What pushed me in the end to defy the received wisdom was the utter boredom of my situation at The Cloisters. I needed work. I could not see that I should be any worse off working for nothing in Jowitt's chambers than I should be in working for nothing at The Cloisters. At No. 1 Brick Court I should have a spacious room to myself overlooking the entrance to Middle Temple Hall and beyond that on the Temple Gardens to the River and the use of William's stenographer, Miss Jones, whom he personally used very little. She was an excellent typist and the notes became quite works of art. There were one or two occasions when William was pressed when he would open a case entirely from my note having hardly looked at the papers.

I did not foresee the immense pleasure that I should get in working with William. Working with him I learnt infinitely more than I could possibly have learnt in any other way and, though the work was hard, every day was full of pleasure. There would moreover be a resumption of those delightful country weekends at Budd's, where Lesley was the perfect hostess and frequently there were interesting guests.

Cheeseman proved very resourceful although there was no question about my being paid anything much. But there was one loophole of which Cheeseman made full use. This was that in addition to the junior, a barrister might be briefed 'to take a note'. No doubt a little longhand note was very useful in the days when shorthand was not practised. But in the thirties shorthand writers were always available and were willing, if required, to provide a note not only of the evidence but also of counsel's speeches. Nevertheless the practice of giving a noting brief was not abandoned. In a large case, Cheeseman developed it with skill. Frequently solicitors who had delivered a brief and had had the preliminary consultation with Sir William, would ask to see him to discuss some minor point that had arisen. As William was in court all morning and most of the afternoons were booked for consultation, it might be a long time before they could get an appointment. 'But', Cheeseman would say, 'Mr Devlin who has been devilling the case for Sir William and is very familiar with it might be able to help you.' The solicitor might have remembered Mr Devlin from the preliminary consultation as looking quite serviceable. Frequently they said yes.

Then I had a few genuine clients like Bischoff Cox. My wife had £500-£600 a year of her own and also worked for Professor Hogben[1], who was researching into identical twins. So we never felt the pinch of stringent economy. It is fair to say that these noting briefs never produced any permanent clients. The instructing solicitors were pleased with the work I did but it never occurred to any of them that

[1] Lancelot Hogben, FRS, then Professor of Social Biology, London University.

they might be equally pleased with the result of any work they sent me on my own. It was ingrained in them that barristers who devilled for silks were in a different class from junior barristers generally and ought not to be allowed to mingle with them. There was only one exception to this rule.

Thomas Cooper was one of the leading firms in the commercial court - or 'list' as it was then called. For the most part the list was made up of cases which were concerned with trade by sea which was still predominantly in British ships. This involved the charter party, the bill of lading and the c.i.f. (cost insurance freight) and f.o.b. (free on board) contracts. This resulted in a great deal of nautical jargon but if you kept firmly in mind the fundamental principles of contract law, 'dejargonisation' was quite easy. The work was almost entirely in the hands of a few solicitors who did little else and of the one or two sets of chambers which were likewise specialised.

Thomas Cooper had a connection with Stibard Gibson, another firm of solicitors through which they did non-commercial work of all sorts including divorce. In those days there was no legal aid. There were what were then known as Poor Persons' cases in which solicitors and counsel gave their services free. All the young barristers did this since it was one of the few ways in which they could have the experience of actually standing up in court and doing a case. But Poor Persons do their best to keep clear of the law. The list consisted almost entirely of P.P.D.s (Poor Persons' Divorces). I was on the list of barristers and Stibard Gibson on the list of solicitors. The managing clerk, who handled the smaller litigation of both firms, was Mr Orchard. One of the cases which came to me was a great rarity, a nullity case which was defended. I did the case to Mr Orchard's satisfaction. Instead of saying to himself 'Here is a man who did a matrimonial case quite well; I shall send him some more', Mr Orchard took a gigantic leap and said to himself 'Here is a man who did not seem to know much about divorce but who did the case quite well; perhaps if I gave him a commercial case he would do that also quite well.' In this way I made my entry into the commercial Bar and eventually acquired a substantial junior practice there. It is the only incidence I know of *a priori* reasoning by a solicitor!

More important than this I had another piece of clear, undiluted luck.

One morning, I think in 1935, Cheeseman placed on my desk with a triumphant air a large brief. Every brief that I had had until then consisted of foolscap folded in half and tied around with red tape (white tape if it was a treasury brief). There is a limit to the number of sheets of paper that can conveniently be handled in this way. In the larger brief, the sort that William had, the papers were kept flat, piled on top of each other and secured by tape not just tied round the middle but top and bottom as well as each side. This brief was secured in that way and stood six or seven inches thick. It came from a firm of solicitors called Walton which, Cheeseman said, had a small but very reputable practice in commercial cases. It was a brief to advise in consultation with Mr Tristram Beresford K.C. and Mr Andrews Uthwatt.

I naturally assumed that my name and fame had spread much further than I had supposed. I had heard the name of Tristram Beresford and I knew a little bit more about Andrews Uthwatt. He was a busy chancery junior. John Brunyate, a Cambridge acquaintance, had gone to him as a pupil and been asked to stay on in chambers. At Cambridge, Brunyate was a close friend of Jack Hamson of whom I have written.[1] They were both persons of the highest class who got firsts in classics and then firsts in law. Brunyate had decided to go the Bar; he had an uncle I think who was a partner in Coward Chance, a leading firm of solicitors in London[2] and Jack was prospering in his academic career.

The plaintiff, Mr Glad, owned a small garage in Denmark and had, so he said, been defrauded by some Americans who operated under the name of Crusader and had tied him up in some way. He wanted to sue for fraud and breach of contract and we were to advise him upon his prospects of success. The solicitors, Geoffrey Perry, a partner, and Mr Marshall, a managing clerk of high dignity and competence, were present but the man who talked most - whose role I did not at first understand and who was addressed familiarly by Andrews Uthwatt as Joe – seemed to be concerned only in a benevolent way. He had clearly made up his mind that Mr Glad should go to law and the only question was how. I supposed that it would be an action in Chancery. Since they had already a leading Chancery junior, it was not clear what my role would be. It transpired that Joe Boyle and Andrews Uthwatt had between them already decided this. They wanted trial by jury so that the action would have to be in the King's Bench. Tristram Beresford was a friend of Uthwatt's and that was why he had been chosen as a good knockout advocate. Uthwatt himself did not intend to appear in the case and so they needed a junior and that was me. Why me? I did not find out until some time later and saw no reason at this stage to explore the mouth of the gift horse. So it was rapidly settled that an action should be launched. I was instructed to draft a statement of claim and it was arranged that the solicitors and the mysterious Mr Boyle should come to my chambers forthwith to discuss it.

As the case proceeded I learnt in little bits the answers to the questions I have mentioned though it was a very long time before I heard the whole of the background.

---

[1] See page 70.

[2] Eventually becoming Clifford Chance, which in 1992 was the largest firm of solicitors in Britain.

The real plaintiff was the Anglo-Saxon petroleum company, a subsidiary of Shell and its main litigating arm. Shell now has, I do not doubt, a large litigation department. In 1930 it had only Mr Boyle. He was a Canadian and litigation was by no means his chief business. He was not a lawyer but he had always been interested in the law and so had come to be relied upon by the Managing Directors in legal matters so that it had come about that he handled all of them. His way of doing business was very informal and he managed to break through many of the conventions of the time which hedged the approach of the client to the barrister. His first hurdle was to find a barrister (he had no use for solicitors as intermediaries) who was prepared to collaborate. This he found in Andrews Uthwatt, an Australian born and bred, who had been educated at Geelong in Australia and who, like himself despised and evaded the conventional. Uthwatt combined a very good legal mind with a very sound practical knowledge of chancery law. But he was no advocate and Joe never trusted him to appear in court. But of his legal wisdom there was no doubt.

I had supposed that Mr Glad was a small struggling man whom the large benevolence of Shell was willing to help and anxious to see that he got his rights. In the eighteenth century that would have given rise no doubt to questions of maintenance, if not of champerty[1] but in the twentieth century they were unlikely to arise. Mr Glad's grievances were quite genuine but Shell was not purely philanthropic. It had found that its efforts to sell petrol in Denmark were being frustrated by what they called piracy. Piracy was committed in their view whenever some small concern started to interfere with the monopolies enjoyed in Europe by the large companies. This was what the defendants, Davis and the Crusader company which he had formed for the purpose, were trying to do. Perhaps if they had stopped there they would not have created so much indignation in the breast of Joe Boyle. But Joe was not merely a Canadian but also an Irish- Canadian and this man Davis was extending his operations into Ireland. Joe certainly believed that Davis was a crook and the thought of letting a crook loose in the mother country was too much for him. Shell managers in Denmark were instructed to report to him any discreditable tales that they heard about Mr Davis and this was how it came to the knowledge of Shell. Joe thought that the most effective way of stopping the piracy was to show how Mr Glad had been treated. It would take some time for litigation to get started and hit the public eye. But if a printed statement of claim could be circulated in Ireland containing an account of Mr Davis's misdeeds it might well put a stop to it.

This was highly improper: a statement of claim is a privileged document.

[1] Champerty:- The illegal proceeding whereby a party not naturally concerned in a suit engages to help one of the litigants to prosecute it, on condition that, in the event of success he is to receive a share of the property in dispute.

Otherwise it might well contain statements on which a libel action could be founded. Of course litigants do show statements of claim to people whom they think might be interested and it may be that circulation was very discreet but it did mean that Shell did not much care whether the action was won or lost and this was an aspect that at the time I never really grasped in full.

I came to the conclusion, probably after I had considered my advice on evidence, that we would be likely to lose on the charge of fraud. So I wrote to Joe Boyle and told him this, saying that I thought he ought to know that my opinion, after seeing all the papers, was that we had a good claim for breach of contract but a doubtful claim in fraud: a loss on the fraud claim might pull the contract claim down with it. Joe wrote back to the effect that there were other considerations to be taken into account.

He was certainly right in thinking that in a jury trial it would be difficult to succeed in one and fail on the other. We did not however get a jury. The defendants, who were of course entitled to a jury as of right, opposed it on the ground of complexity. Nevertheless we won on both heads.

This was a great triumph for Raymond Evershed who had been taken in as leader in place of Beresford. But the defendants took it to appeal. There they were at a disadvantage since the judge had heard the defendant's witnesses and disbelieved them. Harry Willink[1] led for the defence. For five days he seemed to be battling in vain and then on the fifth day and almost during the last words of his speech the tide turned. When it turns as late as that it is unlikely to turn again and so it proved.

We went to the House of Lords to get leave to appeal. Lord Atkin was presiding over the committee. Hardly had Raymond opened his mouth before Atkin said, 'So the defendants having been acquitted of fraud you want to get us to reverse it, do you?'

If Lord Atkin had not been a great judge he would have made an excellent perverse jury man. He turned down leave to appeal so my advice was vindicated.

It was a long time before I learnt how I had been chosen and I was on very friendly terms with Joe before I was told. As I have said, when I first saw the brief I naturally assumed that my name and fame had spread much further than I had supposed. It had not been quite like that: Joe, mindful of his scheme, had looked down a list of practising juniors and chosen the one he thought had the most Irish name - just sheer undiluted luck.

Its consequence was that I got immediately most of Shell's common law litigation in 1941. Andrews Uthwatt was elevated to the Bench and I then succeeded to the whole of the Shell work, not without a little difficulty. Waltons, Shell's solicitors, were horrified that a man of my age should be given such

[1] He later became Master of Magdalen, Cambridge.

responsibility. They conveyed their views to Joe Boyle who reported them to the managing directors.

Joe then said that he would like to give a luncheon to Uthwatt to mark his elevation to the Bench to which he would invite the managing directors and also myself as a potential successor. I did not know that he had any particular purpose in mind and lunch is always a difficult meal for a barrister. I said I would come if I were not in court and Joe said that he would like it very much if I were there.

I understood this better when I found myself sitting next to Sir Frederick Godber, the senior managing director, with whom I got on very well. I remained as counsel to Shell and gave satisfaction . On two occasions I reached what was in those days the accolade of a thousand guinea brief.

Luck at the Bar is opportunity. It is a try that can be converted into a goal.....

POSTSCRIPT

Patrick's goal became his destiny. Years later in 1980, dedicating the law building at St Louis University, USA, he told his audience:

'For almost every man there is a divinity, even if it be only the divinity that shapes his ends. To have an end is to have a destiny. From the belief in a destiny for the human race there springs the drive to march towards it. On the march there must be kept the discipline of the law, an easy discipline when there is that fellow-feeling which is the manifestation of charity.

So let those whose faith is surest and most ardent be in the front ranks, but let them not reject the company of those who believe little because they know not what to believe. As the passport on the march it is enough to have faith in the great commandment, to obey the law that comes out of it and to have hope that in the end virtue will triumph.

Faith, hope, and charity; if a man has these, he is good. And every good man has a God. And every such man can take to himself the words of the Prophet, so fitting in particular for us, whose life is in the law, the words of the Prophet Micah: 'He hath shewed thee, O Man, what is good; and what doth the Lord require of thee, but to do justly, and to love mercy, and to walk humbly with thy God.'

EPILOGUE

PATRICK DEVLIN was a quite exceptional man in so many ways. His charm concealed, at times, an Olympian mind. This, coupled with his steely determination in his pursuit of justice, led to him being so very highly regarded not only within the law but well beyond its confines. Indeed, Lord Scarman has described him as the greatest jurist of all time produced by English Common Law.

In 1986 he joined what had come to be known as the Deputation – Lords Scarman, Jenkins of Hillhead, Merlyn-Rees and myself. We had all come together of our own volition, and each for our own reasons, sharing the belief that there had been a miscarriage of justice in the cases of the Guildford Four and the Maguire Seven. I soon learnt to respect Lord Devlin not only as an outstanding servant of the law, but also a man of great wisdom and integrity in carrying out his professional duties.

The Deputation met regularly between 1986 and 1992 and we set ourselves, as a first task, the securing of a reference back to the Court of Appeal of the Guildford Four case. Patrick Devlin played a major part in the preparation of the submission we presented to the Home Secretary in July 1987. Following that, the submission was developed by him as the prime author, but in conjunction with Lord Scarman, into a compelling article – *"Justice and the Guildford Four"*. The article was so all-embracing and well-argued that *The Times* agreed to publish it in full on 30 November 1988, even though that meant clearing the whole of the left hand centre page. It set out succinctly, and with exceptional clarity, the history of the case including the trial, the Appeal in 1977 which was rejected, and also a major point of law which was of particular concern to Patrick Devlin.

The issue was what the legal system should do with evidence which comes to light after the trial is over. At the Appeal in 1977 four new witnesses (the Balcombe Street Gang) appeared who had committed twenty massacres of the same type. They said they had bombed Guildford but knew nothing of the Guildford Four. The Court of Appeal accepted some of their evidence but not all of it. Lord Devlin's view was that whether or not those four witnesses were lying was a question for a jury to decide.

To his last days, he maintained that on that occasion the Court of Appeal had made an error in law in putting a value themselves on the new evidence. As he put it – "The sleep of the final verdict is disturbed by the nightmare of miscarriage". If his view had prevailed, history might well have been very different.

After the quashing of the convictions of the Guildford Four by the Court of

Appeal in October 1989, Lord Devlin attended fewer meetings of the Deputation as his hearing was rapidly failing. He more than compensated for this by an increased flow of brilliantly argued and beautifully written letters relating to the Maguire Seven case, and to our submissions to the May Inquiry and the Royal Commission on Criminal Justice.

He was profoundly disturbed by the string of miscarriages of justice which followed the quashing of the convictions of the Guildford Four and the Maguire Seven. He acknowledged that the Criminal Justice System had shown itself to be capable of making serious mistakes and he reinforced, with powerful arguments, the Deputation's exposition that there was a need for a new body, independent of Government and the police, to investigate possible miscarriages of justice. As *The Guardian* observed – "In his writings he became to the law what in some ways the Jesuits are to Rome; a rigorous conscience".

His many letters over this period revealed a Christian belief in the centrality of truth, justice and compassion. He had been educated by the Jesuits at Stonyhurst but left early, to enter the Dominican Order as a novice. After six months he decided he would prefer to try to be a secular priest. He then abandoned that course after a year and finally went up to Christ's College, Cambridge, in 1923 to read history and law. No one knows to this day why he left the Dominicans or gave up pursuing the secular priesthood.

At Cambridge he quickly became much taken up with University affairs, was a leading light in the Debating Society and became President of the Union in 1926 in succession to the late Archbishop Ramsey, former Archbishop of Canterbury.

Although while at Cambridge, and seemingly thereafter until near the end, he did not pursue his faith ardently, he never lost his Catholicity as such. This is witnessed by many of his lectures and writings. He met Madeleine in 1931, they were married in 1932, and during the period 1939-1946 four sons and twin daughters were born. At varying times after 1956 Madeleine, and all six of the children, became Roman Catholics.

His family life meant a very great deal to him and he was so well supported and cared for by his wife to his dying days. She told me that towards the end of his life he was given to much thinking for very long periods. After some time, he asked to see a priest. At the very end, some weeks later, he was fortified by the Rites of the Church but declined to take Holy Communion – "because I am not worthy" he said.

An all-loving and all-forgiving God will be the best judge of that.

Cardinal Basil Hume
Archbishop of Westminster

October 1996

PATRICK DEVLIN 1905–1992

1905	Born, Chislehurst, Kent, the second of 5 children
1909	Family moves to Aberdeen. Educated at local convent school
1914-18	Stonyhurst Preparatory School (Hodder)
1918-22	Stonyhurst
1923-27	Christ's College, Cambridge History Part 1 Tripos. Law Part II
1925	American debating tour
1926	President of the Cambridge Union
1927	Works for Arthur Goodhart on *Law Quarterly Review* Apprenticed to Withers, Benson, Currie & Williams
1928	Serves as judge's marshal on Northern Circuit
1929	Called to the Bar and serves Pupillage
1929-31	Devils for Sir William Jowitt, Attorney-General
1930	Practises on Western Circuit
1930	R101 enquiry
1931-39	Prosecuting Counsel to the Mint
1931	Junior Counsel in Hearn murder trial
1931	Kylsant fraud case
1932	Marries Madeleine Oppenheimer
1932	Goes into William Jowitt's Chambers at No. 1 Brick Court
1935	Glad Case (end of Patrick's autobiography) leads to legal work for Shell
1939-46	During these years four sons and twin daughters were born
1940-42	Junior Counsel to the Ministries of War Transport, Food and Supply
1942-45	Legal Department of Ministry of Supply
1943	Buys West Wick House and Farm in Wiltshire
1945	Takes Silk
1947	Appointed a Master of the Bench, Gray's Inn
1947-48	Attorney-General Duchy of Cornwall

1948	Appointed High Court Judge – at 42 one of the two youngest judges to be appointed this century, the other being Charles (later Lord) Hodson
1953-59	Chairman of Council of Bedford College, London University
1955-71	Chairman of Wiltshire Quarter Sessions
1955-56	Chairman of Committee of Inquiry into Dock Labour Scheme
1956-60	President of the Restrictive Practices Court
1956	Publishes *Trial by Jury*
1957	Tries Bodkin Adams
1957	Publishes *The Criminal Prosecution in England*
1959	Chairman of Nyasaland Inquiry Commission
1960-61	Appointed Lord Justice of Appeal
1961-64	Lord Justice of Appeal in Ordinary
1962-76	President, British Maritime Law Association
1962	Publishes *Samples of Lawmaking*
1962	Hon LLD Glasgow University
1962	Hon LLD Toronto University
1963	Treasurer of Gray's Inn
1963	Fellow of British Academy
1964	Retires from being a judge
1964-65	Chairman of Committee of Inquiry into the Port Transport Industry
1964-69	Chairman of the Press Council – first lay chairman
1964-86	Judge of the Administrative Tribunal of the ILO
1965-69	Chairman of the Joint Board for the National Newspaper Industry
1965	Publishes *Enforcement of Morals*
1965	Hon DCL Oxford University
1966	Hon LLD Cambridge University
1966	Hon LLD Leicester University
1966	Hon LLD Sussex University

1966-91	High Steward, Cambridge University
1968	Hon LLD Durham University
1969-71	Chairman of ILO's Inquiry into Freedom of Association in Greece
1970	Hon LLD Liverpool University
1971-72	Chairman of Commission of Inquiry into Industrial Representation
1972	Inquiry into the Student's Sit-in at The Old Schools, Cambridge University
1974-76	Chairman of Committee of Identification in Criminal Cases
1974	Publishes *Too Proud to Fight: Woodrow Wilson's Neutrality*
1979	Publishes *The Judge*
1980	Hon LLD St Louis University
1985	Publishes *Easing the Passing: The Trial of Dr John Bodkin Adams*
1987	Joins Cardinal Hume's campaign for release of Guildford Four
1988	Publishes *The Jury in Two Constitutions*
1988	Begins work on *Taken at the Flood*
1992	Dies at West Wick

INDEX OF NAMES AND PUBLICATIONS